道 *Tao Te Ching*

Tao Te Ching

LAO TZU

道德經

TRANSLATED BY JAMES LEGGE

Foreword by Livia Kohn, Ph.D.

M

METRO BOOKS
NEW YORK

METRO BOOKS
122 FIFTH AVENUE
NEW YORK, NEW YORK 10011

ISBN-13: 978-1-4351-0743-4
Printed and bound in China

10 9 8 7 6 5 4 3 2 1

道德經

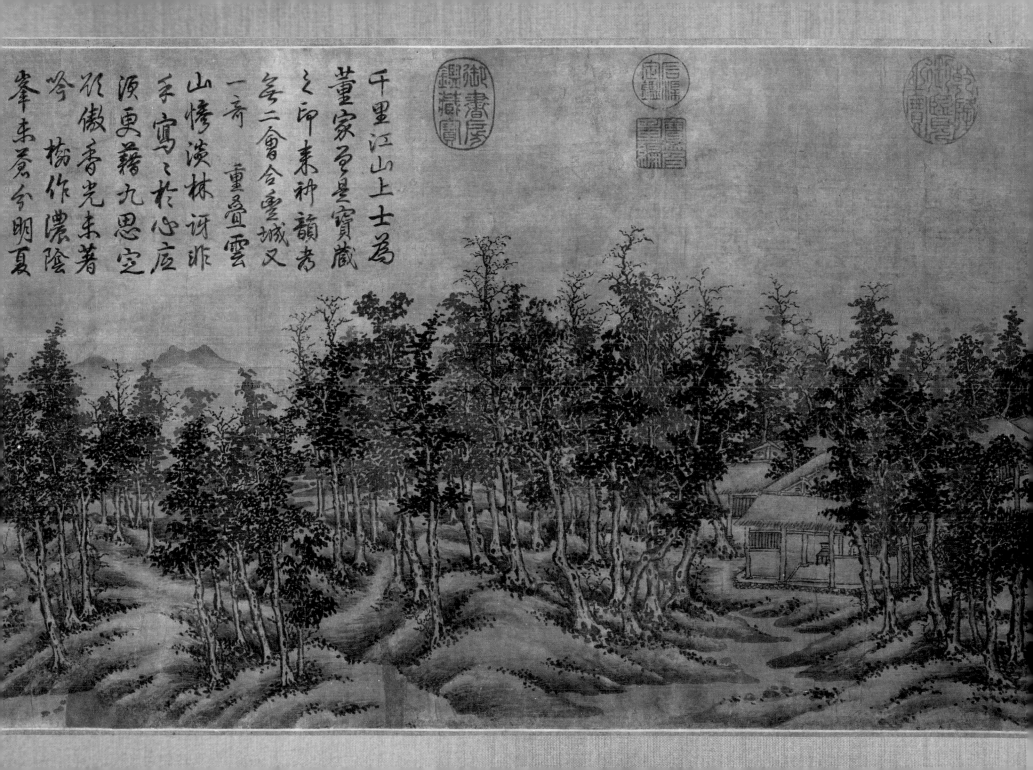

Foreword

The *Tao Te Ching* (*Daode jing*), the "Book of the Way and Its Power," has come to us from troubled times. Compiled around 300 B.C.E., it reflects the key concerns of people thrown into a new and different world, a world much larger and more complex than anything that had gone before. As cultures everywhere adapted to the changes brought by Iron Age technology, China too saw its share of transformation: iron ploughshares afforded a higher quality of plowing and massively increased food production, leading to a population explosion of unprecedented dimension; iron axles for wheels and wagons allowed greater stability and durability of vehicles, creating new horizons of commerce and tremendous wealth for large portions of the population; and—last but not least—weapons made from iron multiplied the destructive power of the military, so that fighting became much more widespread. For the first time in Chinese history, young men were conscripted in great numbers and large infantry armies were set against each other, leading to more or less continuous strife among various feudal states. The latter still pledged formal allegiance to the Zhou court but were in fact independent entities, waging war at the whim of power-hungry rulers and disregarding the civilities of old as much as the well-being of their populace. For good reason, therefore, the time in which the *Tao Te Ching* first appears is called the Warring States Period—a time of upheaval, transformation, and insecurity.

The purpose of the text, which consists of eighty-one short stanza-like chapters written in a form of classical poetry not unlike that of the *Book of Songs*, is accordingly to map out a way in which a person—both an individual caught in the changes and a ruler masterminding them—could retain a sense of harmony, wholeness, and integrity in the whirlwind of a new, often chaotic, and violent world. Its advice is to go back to the source, to come home to an inner ground—called Tao (Dao)—that is stable and predictable; to accept the nature of life and world as constantly changing and refrain from trying to keep it from going in one direction or another; to relax into naturalness, pure organic so-being, a state of letting go or "non-action." Its advice is often geared to counteract dominant tendencies: the push for more, be it status, wealth, or power; the urge to win and dominate and be strong; the need to excel and always be at the top. Quietude and simplicity, softness and weakness, letting go and going with the flow are ideals expressed time and again, joined by visions of small, unified communities where people could live out their lives in simple contentment.

The quest for a way to personal and political harmony is at the root of all Chinese philosophy of the time: the Confucian way of social hierarchies and ethical rules; the Legalist system of control through laws and draconian punishments; the Cosmologists' pursuit of celestial signs and seasonal patterns as a model for human actions and an orderly society. It is also, in different modes and varied visions, at the root of philosophies in other parts of the world: Buddhist liberation through moral behavior and the discipline of the mind; Hindu (Upanishadic) visions of complete freedom from earthly woes; Plato's realm of ideas and his understanding of the good. The awareness that the world is changing and that people matter— how they think, how they act, what they work for—is thus the foundation of all kinds of thought in this Axial Age, a time when humanity first rose to experience the fullness of individual consciousness, gradually replacing tribal and clan-based thinking.

The works of these thinkers still speak to us today, but none more poignantly than the *Tao Te Ching*. We, too, live in troubled times, marked by great technological advances, the globalization of economy and culture, the rise of terrorism, and a marked increase in communal unpredictability and personal insecurity.

The text's emphasis on calmness, quietude, and intuition thus appeals to modern people constantly subjected to the push for increased consumption, i.e., the urge to always have more. When the text says "know when it is enough," we understand that there is a level of material wealth and internal satisfaction that requires one to relax into the present moment and let go of advancement and progress. There is a point when an increase in consumption, a rise in position, or a multiplication of wealth will add nothing further to one's community status or internal well-being but only create complications and difficulties that make one feel worse, not better.

Even this, however, is not stable or permanent but part of universal change, the "continuous alternation of yin and yang." Understanding the world as moving in an ongoing flow of rise and fall, of increase and decline, we can be released from the tension of control and of always doing better. Understanding that too much growth will result in reduction and that a period of calmness and apparent stagnation is the beginning of a new surge of energy, we can make wise decisions. This, in turn, allows us to relax into a state of "non-action," a way of being that lets the flow of nature move at its own pace and in its own way. Listening to the text of the *Tao Te Ching*, enjoying its calming message, we can apply its principles to relationships, parenting, careers, business, and much more. In parenting, for example, we may learn to allow children to make their own discoveries, develop their talents, and grow at their own rate. In business, we may accept that endeavors have a dynamic of their own, moving along with the market and matching popular needs. Instead of being constantly on the move, trying to control and manage everything, the text teaches us to step back and let things unfold naturally. Matching activities to the dominant patterns of the time, "do nothing and there is nothing that is not done."

Doing nothing also means being patient and making small efforts toward big goals—as the text says: "The journey of a thousand leagues commenced with a single step." It means cultivating gentleness and kindness, a laid-back ease, an inner sense of fluidity, expressed as embracing "weakness and softness." And it means being alert to one's true feelings, honest with oneself, and reliable in relations with others, paying more attention to substance than appearances. As the text says: "Sincere words are not fine; fine words are not sincere." Another Chinese proverb that expresses a similar idea is: "Dogs are not considered good if they are good at barking."

ancient Chinese, matching Tao with God: like the early Greek concept of Logos, Tao conveyed the triple sense of supreme being, reason, and word. The first English translation by James Legge (1831–1905) appeared in 1891. It, too, attempted to impose Christian theology onto the Chinese text. This changed in the course of the twentieth century, so that by the end of World War II a number of translations and interpretations had appeared that attempted to read the text in its own right and do justice to Chinese thinking. Since then numerous further renditions have been published, reflecting the timelessness of the text's vision and the continued importance of its message.

There are vast differences among translations of the *Tao Te Ching*. This is partly because of the terse, aphoristic nature of the text, which often leaves out pronouns and grammatical particles. In addition, language in ancient China was not yet standardized, so different characters that had the same sound (homophones) were sometimes used for the same word, creating potential confusion. Also, key words often had a wide range of meanings, leaving it to the reader or translator to make a more or less informed decision. And, finally, uncertainties about syntax abound due to the fact that classical Chinese is uninflected, i.e., it has no specific grammatical endings for gender, plural, or past tense. Each translation thus reflects the preferences and concerns of the translator. Some strive to stick as closely as possible to the original, hoping to achieve a word-for-word rendition that captures the feeling of the text in its original language. Others work to elucidate the historical context and social reality of the original, remaining close to the text but

adding pronouns or prepositions to clarify certain phrases or statements. Such historical translators often use footnotes to amplify and explain the text, placing it within its specific cultural framework. A third type of translation desires to make the text relevant to the modern age. Amplifying the original grammar with pronouns, articles, and other aids, it also employs modern images and concepts that match present-day reality. This kind of translation may be further removed from the original but it carries the strongest resonance with readers today and may, for this very reason, be closer to the original spirit in which the text was conceived.

—Livia Kohn, Ph.D.

Livia Kohn, Ph.D. is Professor Emerita of Religion and East Asian Studies at Boston University. Her specialty is Daoism and the Chinese way of long life. She has written and edited numerous titles and is the editor of the *Journal of Daoist Studies*.

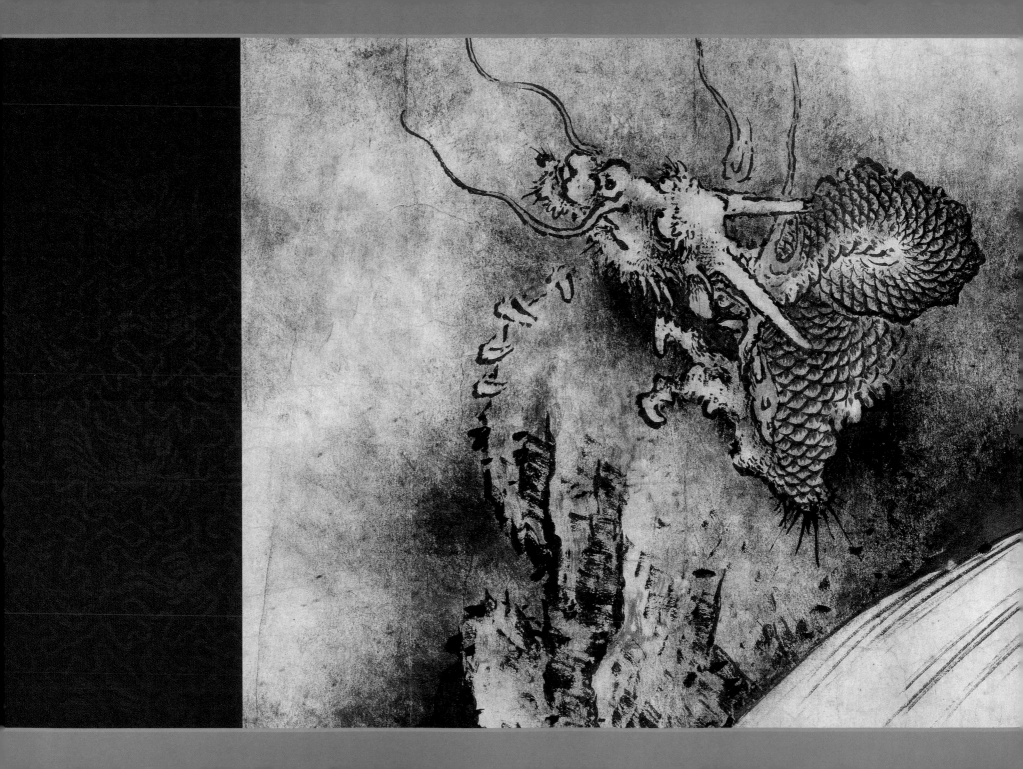

The advice is to look to the quality of the person, not to his or her outward expression, and make sure you yourself express inner sincerity in word and deed.

A similar concept with a slightly different twist is expressed in the text's emphasis on seeing the value of emptiness or what is not there: "Thirty spokes unite in one nave; but it is on the empty space for the axle that the use of the wheel depends." This, as other sayings that speak of the bowl and the bellows, whose empty inner space makes them useful, indicates that one should look beyond the obvious and realize the value of what is not there. This goes for people as much as for spaces, utensils, and business dealings. The person who is quiet and restful often has more to offer than the party lion; a room can be so much more inviting if it is not filled to overflowing; a swimming pool or a tennis court are only effective if they are essentially empty. The Tao itself is said to be ineffable and intangible: if you can describe or name or see it, it is not the Tao. It is the hidden quality at the root of things, the deep sense of cosmic connection, the inherent beauty and goodness in all living beings—felt and sensed only when one steps back from the hustle and bustle of life, when inner calm is found despite the chaos all around.

The person in the *Tao Te Ching* who exemplifies these attitudes and values is the Sage, ideally the ruler, but any individual who follows the principles of the text. Such a person, moreover, will not remain in a vacuum; his or her good values will have a lasting impact on society, creating a sense of stability and harmony wherever he or she goes. This impact begins with the transformation of small communities or social units that develop a model of simple living and show the importance of applying non-action and using resources responsibly. Eventually the process leads to the realization of "naturalness," an overall balance in self, society, and nature. This aspect of the text connects most actively to modern ecology and relates most clearly to visions of environmental harmony and the protection of all species. Although nature in ancient China was seen as more of a threat (with its wild animals and unpredictable weather patterns) than as being threatened, the concept of naturalness ties in closely with the overall attitude of live and let live, of harmony with oneself and with the world at large.

Eighty-one chapters of profound wisdom, concerned with Tao (chapters 1–37) and Virtue (chapters 38–81), are not the work of one man alone. Although transmitted stories tell of a virtuous sage named Lao Tzu (Laozi) who was an archivist in the Zhou capital and the teacher of Confucius (550–579 B.C.E.), and who dictated the words of the *Tao Te Ching* to a border guard on his way into emigration, the text was in fact compiled over a period of decades if not centuries. It is a collection of sayings—aphorisms, poems, proverbs—created and transmitted by likeminded thinkers, people who searched for inner quality and a return to intuitive naturalness in the face of pervasive insecurity. How this happened can only be glimpsed today in evidence provided through archaeological finds.

Thus, in August of 1993, local archaeologists at Guodian (Hubei) unearthed 804 bamboo slips containing roughly 16,000 characters of text. The materials, dated to around 300 B.C.E., contain parts of five ancient philosophical works, including fragments of Confucian and other texts. Among them are thirty-three passages that can be matched with thirty-one chapters of the *Tao Te Ching*, but with lines in different places and considerable variation in characters from the standard, transmitted edition. The fragments are mostly concerned with self-cultivation and its application to questions of rulership and the pacification of the state. They show that the text existed in rudimentary form in the late fourth century, clearly documenting its status as a collection of sayings not yet edited into a coherent presentation. In response to the dire need for order at the time, a set of ideas and practices gradually grew that would eventually develop into something more specifically Taoist.

One hundred fifty years later the text was complete. This is shown in two silk manuscripts excavated in 1973 from a tomb at Mawangdui (Hunan) that was closed in 168 B.C.E. Unlike the earlier bamboo text, this version differs little from the transmitted edition. There are some character variants that have helped clarify some interpretive points, and the two parts are in reversed order, i.e., the text begins with the section on Virtue, then moves to the section on Tao. After this, the text entered a long and varied history of interpretation, allowing numerous thinkers from all sorts of different backgrounds to apply its wisdom to their specific situation and worldview. Most of them followed the standard edition, codified by the erudite Wang Bi (226–249), whose profound and often abstract interpretation has shaped the reception of the text's worldview until today and forms the basis of practically all Western translations.

The first of these was a rendition into Latin by Jesuit missionaries, presented to the British Royal Society in 1788. Its authors hoped to show that the mysteries of the Christian faith were known to the

The Tao

that can

be trodden

is not the

enduring

and

unchanging

Tao.

Absolute

1 *Embodying the Tao*

道可道，非常道。名可名，非常名。無名天地之始。有名

The Tao that can be trodden is not the enduring and unchanging Tao. The name that can be named is not the enduring and unchanging name.

Conceived of as having no name, it is the Originator of Heaven and Earth; conceived of as having a name it is the Mother of all things.

Always without desire we must be found,
if its deep mystery we would sound;
but if desire always within us be,
its outer fringe is all that we shall see.

Under these two aspects, it is really the same; but as development takes place, it receives the different names. Together we call them the Mystery.

Where the Mystery is the deepest, there is the gate of all that is subtle and wonderful.

天下皆知美之爲美斯惡已皆知善之爲善斯不

2 The Nourishment of the Person

All in the world know the beauty of the beautiful, and in doing this they have the idea of what ugliness is; they all know the skill of the skillful, and in doing this they have the idea of what the want of skill is.

So it is that existence and non-existence give birth the one to the idea of the other; that difficulty and ease produce the one the idea of the other; that length and shortness fashion out the one the figure of the other; that the ideas of height and lowness arise from the contrast of the one with the other; that the musical notes and tones become harmonious through the relation of one with another; and that being before and behind give the idea of one following another.

Therefore, the Sage manages affairs without doing anything, and conveys his instructions without the use of speech.

All things spring up, and there is not one which declines to show itself; they grow, and there is no claim made for their ownership; they go through their processes, and there is no expectation of a reward for the results. The work is accomplished, and there is no resting in it as an achievement.

The work is done, but how no one can see;
'tis this that makes the power not cease to be.

3 *Keeping the People at Rest*

不尚賢使民不爭不貴難得之貨使民不爲盜。

Not to value and employ men of superior ability is the way to keep the people from rivalry among themselves; not to prize articles which are difficult to procure is the way to keep them from becoming thieves; not to show them what is likely to excite their desires is the way to keep their minds from disorder.

Therefore, the Sage, in the exercise of his government, empties their minds, fills their bellies, weakens their wills, and strengthens their bones.

He constantly tries to keep them without knowledge and without desire, and where there are those who have knowledge, to keep them from presuming to act on it.

When there is this abstinence from action, good order is universal.

4 The Fountainless

道
冲
而
用
之
或
不
盈
。
淵
今
似
萬
物
之
宗
。
挫
其
銳
。
解

The Tao is like the emptiness of a vessel; and in our employment of it we must be on our guard against all fullness. How deep and unfathomable it is, as if it were the Honored Ancestor of all things!

We should blunt our sharp points, and unravel the complications of things; we should temper our brightness, and bring ourselves into agreement with the obscurity of others. How pure and still the Tao is, as if it would ever so continue!

I do not know whose son it is. It might appear to have been before God.

5 The Use of Emptiness

天
地
不
仁
以
萬
物
爲
芻
狗
。
聖
人
不
仁
以
百
姓
爲

Heaven and Earth do not act from the impulse of any wish to be benevolent; they deal with all things as the dogs of grass are dealt with. The sages do not act from any wish to be benevolent; they deal with the people as the dogs of grass are dealt with.

May not the space between Heaven and Earth be compared to a bellows?

'Tis emptied, yet it loses not its power;
'tis moved again, and sends forth air the more.

Much speech to swift exhaustion lead we see;
your inner being guard, and keep it free.

6 *The Completion of Material Forms*

The valley spirit dies not, aye the same;
the female mystery thus do we name.
Its gate, from which at first they issued forth,
is called the root from which grew Heaven and Earth.

Long and unbroken does its power remain,
Used gently, and without the touch of pain.

谷神不死是謂玄牝玄牝之門是謂天地根綿綿若

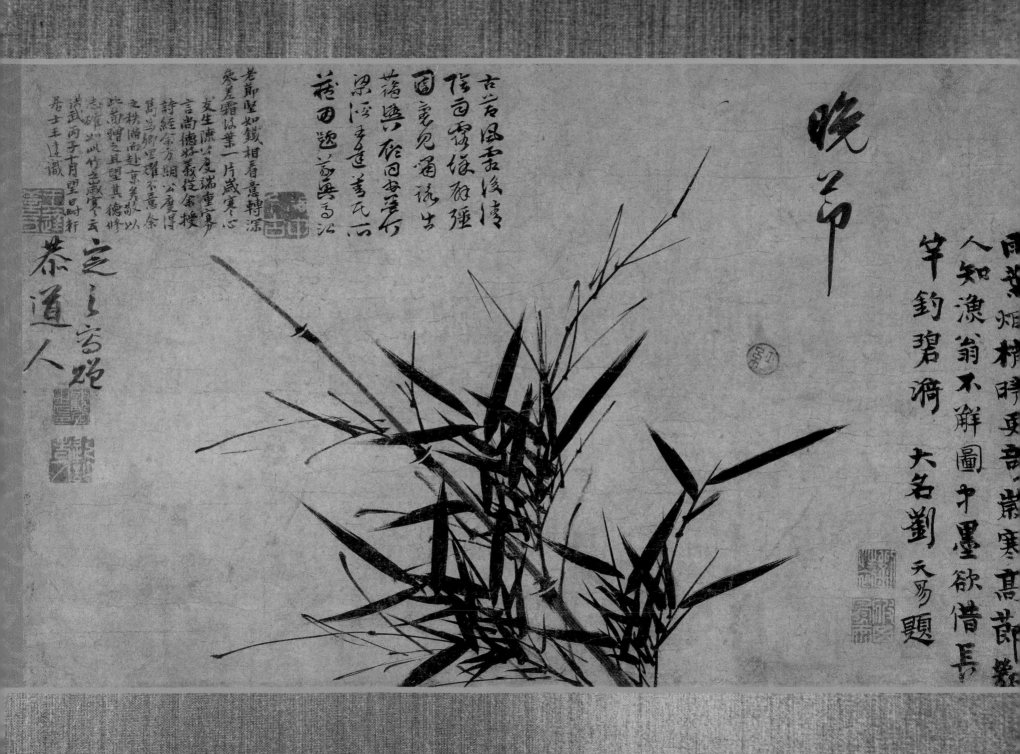

7 Sheathing the Light

天長地久。天地所以能長且久者。以其不自生。

Heaven is long-enduring, and Earth continues long.
The reason why Heaven and Earth are able to endure
and continue thus long is because they do not live of,
or for, themselves. This is how they are able to continue
and endure.

Therefore, the Sage puts his own person last, and yet it is
found in the foremost place; he treats his person as if it were
foreign to him, and yet that person is preserved. Is it not
because he has no personal and private ends, that therefore
such ends are realized?

8 The Placid and Contented Nature

上善若水。水善利萬物而不爭。處眾人之所惡。

The highest excellence is like that of water. The excellence
of water appears in its benefiting all things, and in its
occupying, without striving to the contrary, the low place
which all men dislike. Hence its way is near to that of
the Tao.

The excellence of a residence is in the suitability of the
place; that of the mind is in abysmal stillness; that of
associations is in their being with the virtuous; that of
government is in its securing good order; that of the
conduct of affairs is in its ability; and that of the initiation
of any movement is in its timeliness.

And when one with the highest excellence does not wrangle
about his low position, no one finds fault with him.

9 *Fullness and Complacency Contrary to the Tao*

It is better to leave a vessel unfilled,
than to attempt to carry it when it is full.

If you keep feeling a point that has been sharpened,
the point cannot long preserve its sharpness.

When gold and jade fill the hall, their possessor cannot
keep them safe.

When wealth and honors lead to arrogance,
this brings its evil on itself.

When the work is done, and one's name is becoming
distinguished, to withdraw into obscurity is the way
of Heaven.

持而盈之、不如其已揣而梲之、不可長保。金玉滿

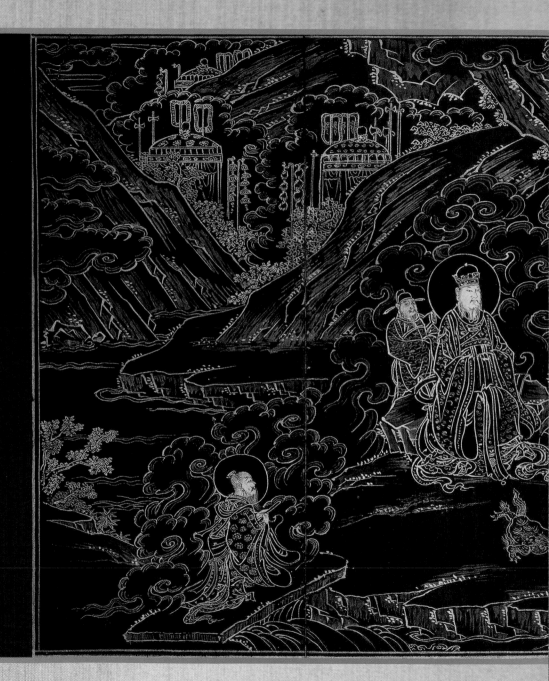

The

Tao

produces

all

things

and

nourishes

them.

Reason

10 Possibilities Through the Tao

載營魄抱一能無離乎專氣致柔能嬰兒乎滌除玄

When the intelligent and animal souls are held together in one embrace, they can be kept from separating. When one gives undivided attention to the vital breath, and brings it to the utmost degree of pliancy, he can become as a tender babe. When he has cleansed away the most mysterious sights of his imagination, he can become without a flaw.

In loving the people and ruling the state, cannot he proceed without any purpose of action? In the opening and shutting of his gates of Heaven, cannot he do so as a female bird? While his intelligence reaches in every direction, cannot he appear to be without knowledge?

The Tao produces all things and nourishes them; it produces them and does not claim them as its own; it does all, and yet does not boast of it; it presides over all, and yet does not control them. This is what is called "The mysterious Quality" of the Tao.

三十輻共一轂當其無有車之用埏埴以爲器當

11 The Use of What Has No Substantive Existence

The thirty spokes unite in the one nave; but it is on the empty space for the axle that the use of the wheel depends.

Clay is fashioned into vessels; but it is on their empty hollowness that their use depends.

The door and windows are cut out from the walls to form an apartment; but it is on the empty space within that its use depends.

Therefore, what has a positive existence serves for profitable adaptation, and what has not that for actual usefulness.

12 *The Repression of the Desires*

Color's five hues from th' eyes their sight will take;
music's five notes the ears as deaf can make;
the flavors five deprive the mouth of taste;
the chariot course, and the wild hunting waste
make mad the mind; and objects rare and strange,
sought for, men's conduct will to evil change.

Therefore, the Sage seeks to satisfy the craving of
the belly, and not the insatiable longing of the eyes.
He puts from him the latter, and prefers to seek
the former.

五色令人目盲。五音令人耳聾。五味令人口爽。馳騁

13 Loathing Shame

寵辱若驚貴大患若身何謂寵辱若驚寵為下得之

Favor and disgrace would seem equally to be feared; honor and great calamity to be regarded as personal conditions of the same kind.

What is meant by speaking thus of favor and disgrace? Disgrace is being in a low position after the enjoyment of favor. The getting of favor leads to the apprehension of losing it, and the losing of it leads to the fear of still greater calamity: This is what is meant by saying that favor and disgrace would seem equally to be feared.

And what is meant by saying that honor and great calamity are to be similarly regarded as personal conditions? What makes me liable to great calamity is my having the body which I call myself; if I had not the body, what great calamity could come to me?

Therefore, he who would administer the kingdom, honoring it as he honors his own person, may be employed to govern it, and he who would administer it with the love which he bears to his own person may be entrusted with it.

李嵩明皇鬥雞圖

14 — The Manifestation of Mystery

視之不見名曰夷。聽之不聞名曰希。搏之不得名曰

We look at it, and we do not see it, and we name it "the Equable."

We listen to it, and we do not hear it, and we name it "the Inaudible."

We try to grasp it, and do not get hold of it, and we name it "the Subtle."

With these three qualities, it cannot be made the subject of description; and hence we blend them together and obtain The One.

Its upper part is not bright, and its lower part is not obscure. Ceaseless in its action, it yet cannot be named, and then it again returns and becomes nothing. This is called the Form of the Formless, and the Semblance of the Invisible; this is called the Fleeting and Indeterminable.

We meet it and do not see its Front; we follow it, and do not see its Back. When we can lay hold of the Tao of old to direct the things of the present day, and are able to know it as it was of old in the beginning, this is called unwinding the clue of Tao.

15 — The Exhibition of the Qualities of the Tao

古之善爲士者微妙玄通深不可識。夫唯不可識故

The skillful masters of the Tao in old times, with a subtle and exquisite penetration, comprehended its mysteries, and were deep also so as to elude men's knowledge.

As they were thus beyond men's knowledge, I will make an effort to describe of what sort they appeared to be.

Shrinking looked they like those who wade through a stream in winter; irresolute like those who are afraid of all around them; grave like a guest in awe of his host; evanescent like ice that is melting away; unpretentious like wood that has not been fashioned into anything; vacant like a valley, and dull like muddy water. Who can make the muddy water clear? Let it be still, and it will gradually become clear. Who can secure the condition of rest? Let movement go on, and the condition of rest will gradually arise.

They who preserve this method of the Tao do not wish to be full of themselves. It is through their not being full of themselves that they can afford to seem worn and not appear new and complete.

致虛極。守靜篤。萬物並作。吾以觀復。夫物芸芸各復

16 *Returning to the Root*

The state of vacancy should be brought to the utmost degree, and that of stillness guarded with unwearying vigor. All things alike go through their processes of activity, and then we see them return to their original state. When things in the vegetable world have displayed their luxuriant growth, we see each of them return to its root. This returning to their root is what we call the state of stillness; and that stillness may be called a reporting that they have fulfilled their appointed end.

The report of that fulfillment is the regular, unchanging rule. To know that unchanging rule is to be intelligent; not to know it leads to wild movements and evil issues. The knowledge of that unchanging rule produces a grand capacity and forbearance, and that capacity and forbearance lead to a community of feeling with all things. From this community of feeling comes a kingliness of character; and he who is king-like goes on to be heaven-like. In that likeness to Heaven he possesses the Tao. Possessed of the Tao, he endures long; and to the end of his bodily life, is exempt from all danger of decay.

17 *The Unadulterated Influence*

In the highest antiquity, the people did not know that there were rulers. In the next age they loved them and praised them. In the next they feared them; in the next they despised them. Thus it was that when faith in the Tao was deficient in the rulers a want of faith in them ensued in the people.

How irresolute did those earliest rulers appear, showing by their reticence the importance which they set upon their words! Their work was done and their undertakings were successful, while the people all said, "We are as we are, of ourselves!"

太上下知有之。其次親而譽之。其次畏之。其次侮之。

18 *The Decay of Manners*

大道廢有仁義慧智出有大僞六親不和有孝慈

When the Great Tao Way or Method ceased to be observed, benevolence and righteousness came into vogue. Then appeared wisdom and shrewdness, and there ensued great hypocrisy.

When harmony no longer prevailed throughout the six kinships, filial sons found their manifestation; when the states and clans fell into disorder, loyal ministers appeared.

奇筆驚天陳所翁
畫龍性許與龍通
劈開礁石倒流水
噴出漱雪浮浩雲
變化老聃猶可肖形

I

am

like an

infant

which

has not

yet

smiled.

Rituals

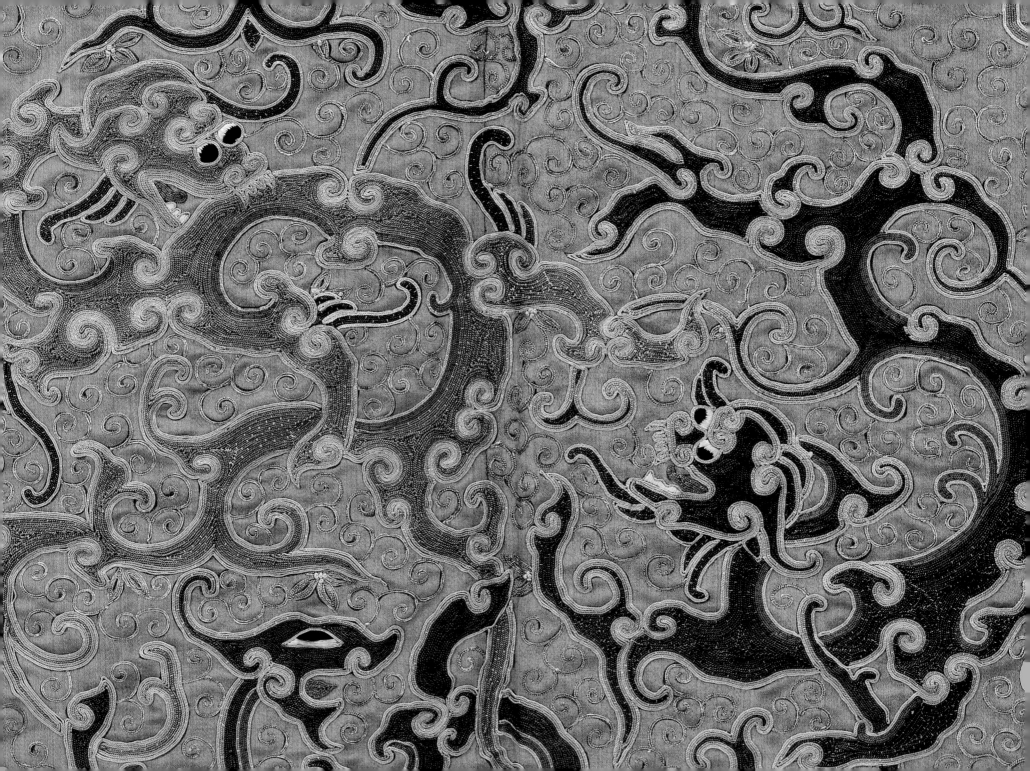

19 Returning to the Unadulterated Influence

絶聖棄智民利百倍絶仁棄義民復孝慈絶巧棄

If we could renounce our sageness and discard
our wisdom, it would be better for the people
a hundredfold.

If we could renounce our benevolence and discard
our righteousness, the people would again become
filial and kindly.

If we could renounce our artful contrivances and
discard our scheming for gain, there would be no
thieves nor robbers.

Those three methods of government
thought olden ways in elegance did fail
and made these names their want of worth to veil;
but simple views, and courses plain and true
would selfish ends and many lusts eschew.

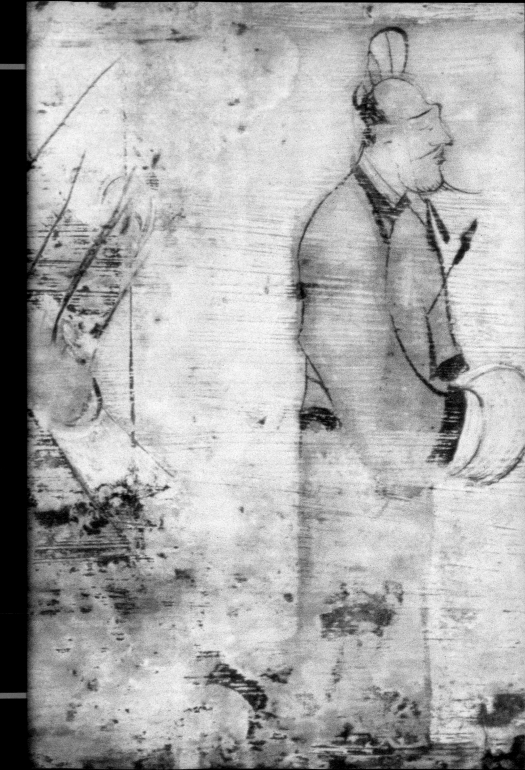

20 Being Different from Ordinary Men

絶
學
無
憂
。
唯
之
與
阿
、
相
去
幾
何
。
善
之
與
惡
相
去
若
何
。

When we renounce learning we have no troubles.

The ready "yes," and flattering "yea";
small is the difference they display.
But mark their issues, good and ill;
what space the gulf between shall fill?

What all men fear is indeed to be feared; but how wide and
without end is the range of questions asking to be discussed!

The multitude of men look satisfied and pleased; as if
enjoying a full banquet, as if mounted on a tower in spring.
I alone seem listless and still, my desires having as yet given
no indication of their presence. I am like an infant which
has not yet smiled. I look dejected and forlorn, as if I had
no home to go to.

The multitude of men all know when it is enough. I alone
seem to have lost everything. My mind is that of a stupid
man; I am in a state of chaos. Ordinary men look bright and
intelligent, while I alone seem to be benighted. They look
full of discrimination, while I alone am dull and confused.
I seem to be carried about as on the sea, drifting as if I had
nowhere to rest.

All men have their spheres of action, while I alone seem dull
and incapable, like a rude borderer. Thus I alone am different
from other men, but I value the nursing-mother: the Tao.

21 The Empty Heart, or the Tao in Its Operation

孔
德
之
容
、
惟
道
是
從
。
道
之
爲
物
惟
恍
惟
惚
。
惚
兮
恍
兮
、

The grandest forms of active force
from Tao come, their only source.
Who can of Tao the nature tell?
Our sight it flies, our touch as well.
Eluding sight, eluding touch,
the forms of things all in it crouch;
eluding touch, eluding sight,
there are their semblances, all right.
Profound it is, dark and obscure;
things' essences all there endure.
Those essences the truth enfold
of what, when seen, shall then be told.
Now it is so; 'twas so of old.
Its name—what passes not away;
so, in their beautiful array,
things form and never know decay.

How know I that it is so with all the beauties of
existing things? By this nature of the Tao.

22 *The Increase Granted to Humility*

曲則全枉則直窪則盈敝則新少則得多則惑是以

The partial becomes complete; the crooked, straight; the empty, full; the worn out, new.

He whose desires are few gets them;
he whose desires are many goes astray.

Therefore, the Sage holds in his embrace the one thing of humility, and manifests it to all the world. He is free from self-display, and therefore he shines; from self-assertion, and therefore he is distinguished; from self-boasting, and therefore his merit is acknowledged; from self-complacency, and therefore he acquires superiority. It is because he is thus free from striving that therefore no one in the world is able to strive with him. That saying of the ancients that "the partial becomes complete" was not vainly spoken: all real completion is comprehended under it.

23 *Absolute Vacancy*

希言自然。故飄風不終朝驟雨不終日。孰爲此者天

Abstaining from speech marks him who is obeying the spontaneity of his nature. A violent wind does not last for a whole morning; a sudden rain does not last for the whole day. To whom is it that these two things are owing? To Heaven and Earth. If Heaven and Earth cannot make such spasmodic actings last long, how much less can man!

Therefore, when one is making the Tao his business, those who are also pursuing it agree with him in it, and those who are making the manifestation of its course their object agree with him in that; while even those who are failing in both these things agree with him where they fail.

Hence, those with whom he agrees as to the Tao have the happiness of attaining to it; those with whom he agrees as to its manifestation have the happiness of attaining to it; and those with whom he agrees in their failure have also the happiness of attaining to the Tao.

But when there is not faith sufficient on his part, a want of faith in him ensues on the part of the others.

24 *Painful Graciousness*

He who stands on his tiptoes does not stand firm; he who stretches his legs does not walk easily. So, he who displays himself does not shine; he who asserts his own views is not distinguished; he who vaunts himself does not find his merit acknowledged; he who is self-conceited has no superiority allowed to him.

Such conditions, viewed from the standpoint of the Tao, are like remnants of food, or a tumor on the body, which all dislike. Hence those who pursue the course of the Tao do not adopt and allow them.

企者不立跨者不行自見者不明自是者不彰自

25 *Representations of the Mystery*

有物混成先天地生寂兮寥兮獨立不改周行而

There was something undefined and complete, coming into existence before Heaven and Earth.

How still it was and formless, standing alone, and undergoing no change, reaching everywhere and in no danger of being exhausted! It may be regarded as the Mother of all things. I do not know its name, and I give it the designation of the Tao. Making an effort further to give it a name I call it The Great.

Great, it passes on in constant flow. Passing on, it becomes remote. Having become remote, it returns.

Therefore, the Tao is great; Heaven is great; Earth is great; and the sage king is also great. In the universe there are four that are great, and the sage king is one of them.

Man takes his law from the Earth; the Earth takes its law from Heaven; Heaven takes its law from the Tao. The law of the Tao is its being what it is.

26 *The Quality of Gravity*

Gravity is the root of lightness;
stillness the ruler of movement.

Therefore a wise prince, marching the whole day, does
not go far from his baggage wagons. Although he may
have brilliant prospects to look at, he quietly remains
in his proper place, indifferent to them.

How should the lord of a myriad chariots carry
himself lightly before the kingdom? If he does act
lightly, he has lost his root of gravity; if he proceeds
to active movement, he will lose his throne.

重爲輕根。靜爲躁君。是以聖人終日行不離輜重。

27 *Dexterity in Using the Tao*

善行無轍迹。善言無瑕讁。善數不用籌策。善閉無關

The skillful traveler leaves no traces of his wheels or footsteps; the skillful speaker says nothing that can be found fault with or blamed; the skillful reckoner uses no tallies; the skillful closer needs no bolts or bars, while to open what he has shut will be impossible; the skillful binder uses no strings or knots, while to unloose what he has bound will be impossible.

In the same way the Sage is always skillful at saving men, and so he does not cast away any man; he is always skillful at saving things, and so he does not cast away anything.

This is called "Hiding the light of his procedure."

Therefore, the man of skill is a master to be looked up to by him who has not the skill; and he who has not the skill is the helper of the reputation of him who has the skill. If the one did not honor his master, and the other did not rejoice in his helper, an observer, though intelligent, might greatly err about them. This is called "The utmost degree of mystery."

A

skillful

commander

strikes

a decisive

blow,

and

stops.

Light

28 *Returning to Simplicity*

知其雄守其雌爲天下谿爲天下谿常德不離復歸

Who knows his manhood's strength,
yet still his female feebleness maintains;
as to one channel flow the many drains,
all come to him, yea, all beneath the sky.
Thus he the constant excellence retains;
the simple child again, free from all stains.

Who knows how white attracts,
yet always keeps himself within black's shade,
the pattern of humility displayed,
displayed in view of all beneath the sky;
he in the unchanging excellence arrayed,
endless return to man's first state has made.

Who knows how glory shines,
yet loves disgrace, nor e'er for it is pale;
behold his presence in a spacious vale,
to which men come from all beneath the sky.
The unchanging excellence completes its tale;
the simple infant man in him we hail.

The unwrought material, when divided and distributed,
forms vessels. The Sage, when employed, becomes the
Head of all the Officers of government; and in his
greatest regulations he employs no violent measures.

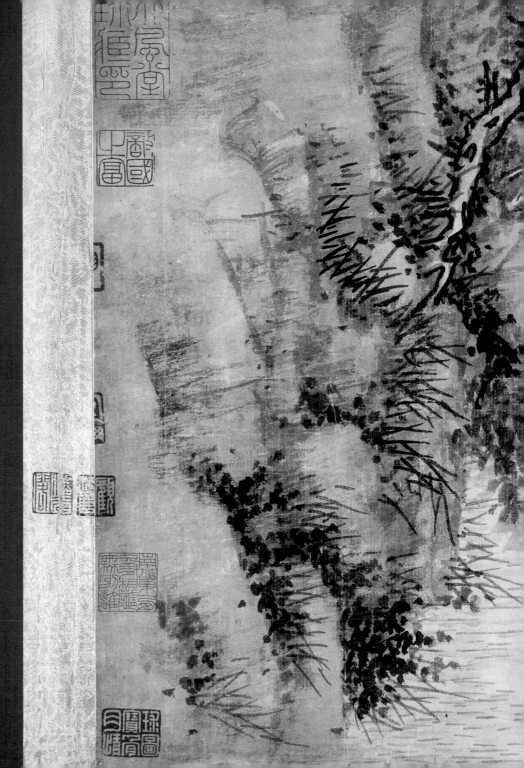

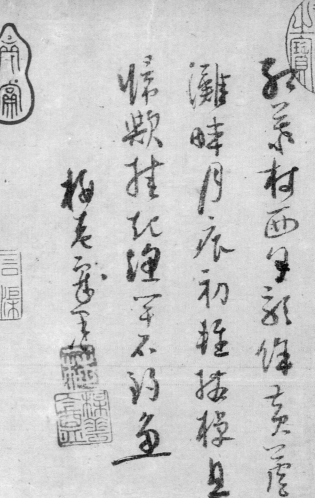

紅蓼村西夕釣停

蘆灘月夜初程搖棹且

慣歌挂花漁笛不鳴魚

柏老墨戲

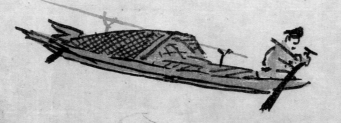

29 *Taking No Action*

将欲取天下而為之吾見其不得已天下神器不可

If anyone should wish to get the kingdom for himself, and to effect this by what he does, I see that he will not succeed.

The kingdom is a spirit-like thing, and cannot be got by active doing. He who would so win it destroys it; he who would hold it in his grasp loses it.

The course and nature of things is such that
what was in front is now behind;
what warmed anon we freezing find.
Strength is of weakness oft the spoil;
the store in ruins mocks our toil.

Hence, the Sage puts away excessive effort, extravagance, and easy indulgence.

30 *A Caveat Against War*

以道佐人主者不以兵强天下其事好還師之所處

He who would assist a lord of men in harmony with the Tao will not assert his mastery in the kingdom by force of arms. Such a course is sure to meet with its proper return.

Wherever a host is stationed, briars and thorns spring up. In the sequence of great armies there are sure to be bad years.

A skillful commander strikes a decisive blow, and stops. He does not dare by continuing his operations to assert and complete his mastery. He will strike the blow, but will be on his guard against being vain or boastful or arrogant in consequence of it. He strikes it as a matter of necessity; he strikes it, but not from a wish for mastery.

When things have attained their strong maturity they become old. This may be said to be not in accordance with the Tao: and what is not in accordance with it soon comes to an end.

31 *Stilling War*

夫佳兵者不祥之器物或惡之故有道者不處君子

Now arms, however beautiful, are instruments of evil omen, hateful, it may be said, to all creatures. Therefore, they who have the Tao do not like to employ them.

The superior man ordinarily considers the left hand the most honorable place, but in time of war the right hand.

Those sharp weapons are instruments of evil omen, and not the instruments of the superior man; he uses them only on the compulsion of necessity. Calm and repose are what he prizes; victory by force of arms is to him undesirable.

To consider this desirable would be to delight in the slaughter of men; and he who delights in the slaughter of men cannot get his will in the kingdom.

On occasions of festivity, to be on the left hand is the prized position; on occasions of mourning, the right hand. The second in command of the army has his place on the left; the general commanding in chief has his on the right; his place, that is, is assigned to him as in the rites of mourning. He who has killed multitudes of men should weep for them with the bitterest grief; and the victor in battle has his place rightly according to those rites.

32 *The Tao with No Name*

道常無名。樸雖小天下莫能臣也。侯王若能守之萬

The Tao, considered as unchanging, has no name. Though in its primordial simplicity it may be small, the whole world dares not deal with one embodying it as a minister. If a feudal prince or the king could guard and hold it, all would spontaneously submit themselves to him. Heaven and Earth under its guidance unite together and send down the sweet dew, which, without the directions of men, reaches equally everywhere as of its own accord.

As soon as it proceeds to action, it has a name. When it once has that name, men can know to rest in it. When they know to rest in it, they can be free from all risk of failure and error.

The relation of the Tao to all the world is like that of the great rivers and seas to the streams from the valleys.

33 *Discriminating Between Attributes*

He who knows other men is discerning;
he who knows himself is intelligent.

He who overcomes others is strong;
he who overcomes himself is mighty.

He who is satisfied with his lot is rich;
he who goes on acting with energy has a firm will.

He who does not fail in the requirements of his position
continues long; he who dies, and yet does not perish,
has longevity.

知人者智。自知者明。勝人者有力。自勝者強。知足者

34 *The Task of Achievement*

大
道
氾
兮
其
可
左
右
。
萬
物
恃
之
而
生
而
不
辭
。
功
成
不

All-pervading is the Great Tao! It may be found on the left hand and on the right.

All things depend on it for their production, which it gives to them, not one refusing obedience to it.

When its work is accomplished, it does not claim the name of having done it.

It clothes all things as with a garment, and makes no assumption of being their lord; it may be named in the smallest things.

All things return to their root and disappear, and do not know that it is it which presides over their doing so; it may be named in the greatest things.

Hence, the Sage is able in the same way to accomplish his great achievements. It is through his not making himself great that he can accomplish them.

35 *The Attribute of Benevolence*

執大象天下往往而不害安平太樂與餌過客止道

To him who holds in his hands the Great Image of the invisible Tao, the whole world repairs. Men resort to him, and receive no hurt, but find rest, peace, and the feeling of ease.

Music and dainties will make the passing guest stop for a time. But though the Tao as it comes from the mouth seems insipid and has no flavor, and though it seems not worth being looked at or listened to, the use of it is inexhaustible.

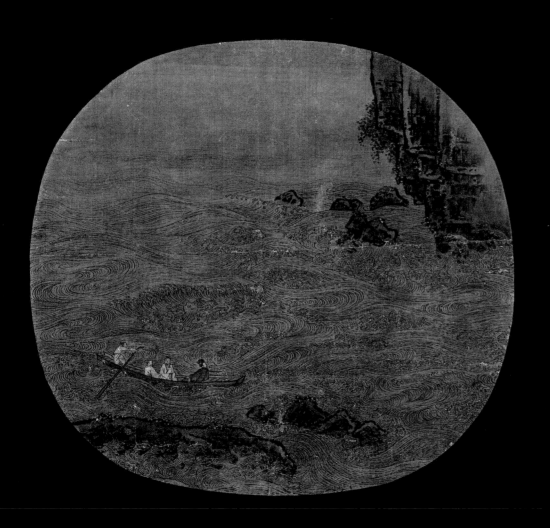

36 *Minimizing the Light*

將欲歙之必固張之。將欲弱之必固強之。將欲廢之

When one is about to take an inspiration, he is sure to make a previous expiration; when he is going to weaken another, he will first strengthen him; when he is going to overthrow another, he will first have raised him up; when he is going to despoil another, he will first have made gifts to him: this is called "Hiding the light of his procedure."

The soft overcomes the hard; and the weak the strong.

Fishes should not be taken from the deep; instruments for the profit of a state should not be shown to the people.

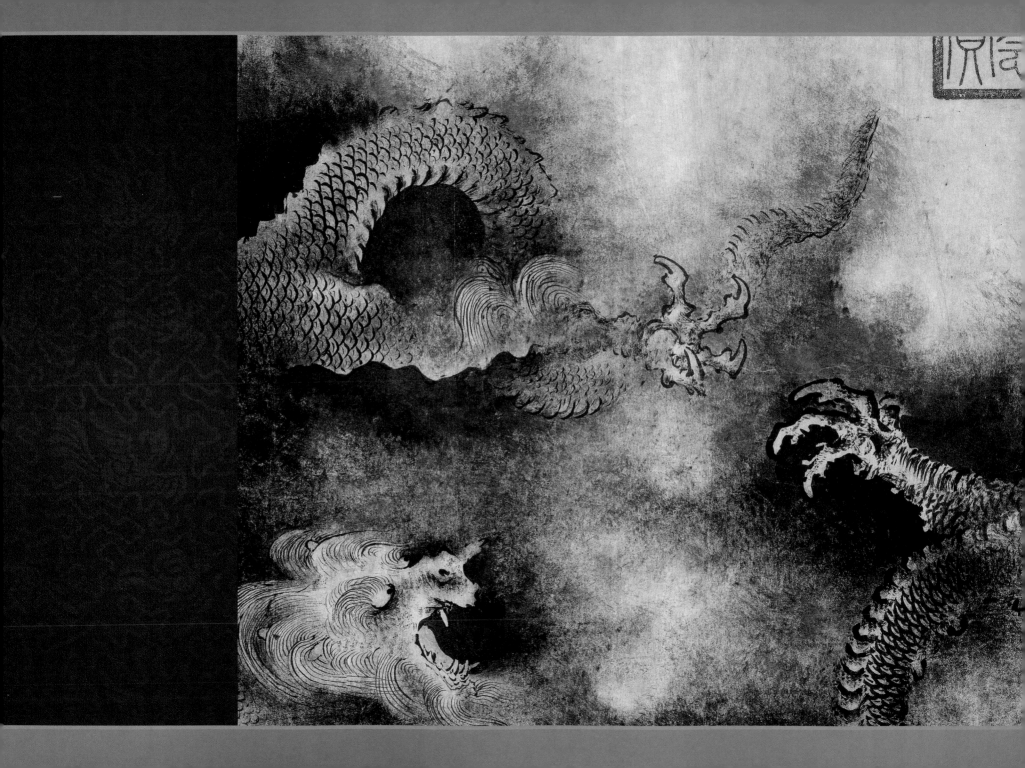

So

it is

that

some

things are

increased

by being

diminished.

Dark

37 The Exercise of Government

The Tao in its regular course does nothing for the sake
of doing it, and so there is nothing which it does not do.
If princes and kings were able to maintain it, all things
would of themselves be transformed by them. If this
transformation became to me an object of desire,
I would express the desire by the nameless simplicity.

Simplicity without a name
is free from all external aim.
With no desire, at rest and still,
all things go right as of their will.

道常無爲而無不爲侯王若能守之萬物將自化。

38 *About the Attributes of the Tao*

上德不德，是以有德。下德不失德，是以無德。上德無

Those who possessed in highest degree the attributes of the Tao did not seek to show them, and therefore they possessed them in fullest measure. Those who possessed in a lower degree those attributes sought how not to lose them, and therefore they did not possess them in fullest measure.

Those who possessed in the highest degree those attributes did nothing with a purpose, and had no need to do anything. Those who possessed them in a lower degree were always doing, and had need to be so doing.

Those who possessed the highest benevolence were always seeking to carry it out, and had no need to be doing so. Those who possessed the highest righteousness were always seeking to carry it out, and had need to be so doing.

Those who possessed the highest sense of propriety were always seeking to show it, and when men did not respond to it, they bared the arm and marched up to them.

Thus it was that when the Tao was lost, its attributes appeared; when its attributes were lost, benevolence appeared; when benevolence was lost, righteousness appeared; and when righteousness was lost, the proprieties appeared.

Now propriety is the attenuated form of leal-heartedness and good faith, and is also the commencement of disorder; swift apprehension is only a flower of the Tao, and is the beginning of stupidity.

Thus it is that the Great man abides by what is solid, and eschews what is flimsy; dwells with the fruit and not with the flower. It is thus that he puts away the one and makes choice of the other.

39 *The Origin of the Law*

昔
之
得
一
者
。
天
得
一
以
清
。
地
得
一
以
寧
。
神
得
一
以
靈
。

The things which from of old have got the One Tao are:
Heaven which by it is bright and pure;
Earth rendered thereby firm and sure;
spirits with powers by it supplied;
valleys kept full throughout their void;
all creatures which through it do live;
princes and kings who from it get;
the model which to all they give.
All these are the results of the One Tao.

If Heaven were not thus pure, it soon would rend;
if Earth were not thus sure, 'twould break and bend;
without these powers, the spirits soon would fail;
if not so filled, the drought would parch each vale;
without that life, creatures would pass away;
princes and kings, without that moral sway,
however grand and high, would all decay.

Thus it is that dignity finds its firm root in its previous meanness, and what is lofty finds its stability in the lowness from which it rises. Hence princes and kings call themselves "Orphans," "Men of small virtue," and as "Carriages without a nave." Is not this an acknowledgment that in their considering themselves mean they see the foundation of their dignity? So it is that in the enumeration of the different parts of a carriage we do not come on what makes it answer the ends of a carriage. They do not wish to show themselves elegant-looking as jade, but prefer to be coarse-looking as an ordinary stone.

40 Dispensing with the Use of Means

反者道之動弱者道之用天下萬物生於有有生於

The movement of the Tao by contraries proceeds;
and weakness marks the course of Tao's mighty deeds.

All things under Heaven sprang from It as existing
and named;
that existence sprang from It as non-existent
and not named.

41 Sameness and Difference

上士聞道勤而行之中士聞道若存若亡下士聞道

Scholars of the highest class, when they hear about the Tao,
earnestly carry it into practice. Scholars of the middle class,
when they have heard about it, seem now to keep it and now
to lose it. Scholars of the lowest class, when they have heard
about it, laugh greatly at it. If it were not thus laughed at,
it would not be fit to be the Tao.

Therefore, the sentence-makers have thus expressed
themselves:
"The Tao, when brightest seen, seems light to lack;
who progress in it makes, seems drawing back;
its even way is like a rugged track.
Its highest virtue from the vale doth rise;
its greatest beauty seems to offend the eyes;
and he has most whose lot the least supplies.
Its firmest virtue seems but poor and low;
its solid truth seems change to undergo;
its largest square doth yet no corner show.
A vessel great, it is the slowest made;
loud is its sound, but never word it said;
a semblance great, the shadow of a shade."

The Tao is hidden, and has no name; but it is the Tao which
is skillful at imparting to all things what they need and
making them complete.

42 The Transformations of the Tao

道生一一生二二生三三生萬物萬物負陰而抱

The Tao produced One; One produced Two; Two produced Three; Three produced All things.

All things leave behind them the Obscurity out of which they have come, and go forward to embrace the Brightness into which they have emerged, while they are harmonized by the Breath of Vacancy.

What men dislike is to be orphans, to have little virtue, to be as carriages without naves; and yet these are the designations which kings and princes use for themselves.

So it is that some things are increased by being diminished, and others are diminished by being increased.

What other men thus teach, I also teach. The violent and strong do not die their natural death. I will make this the basis of my teaching.

宋徽宗摹張萱擣練圖真蹟

金章宗題

禹江邨清吟堂秘藏

天水摹張萱擣練圖

43 The Universal Use of the Action in Weakness of the Tao

The softest thing in the world dashes against and overcomes the hardest; that which has no substantial existence enters where there is no crevice. I know hereby what advantage belongs to doing nothing with a purpose.

There are few in the world who attain to the teaching without words, and the advantage arising from non-action.

天下之至柔馳騁天下之至堅。無有入無間。吾是

44 *Cautions*

Of fame or life, which do you hold more dear?
Of life or wealth, to which would you adhere?
Keep life and lose those other things;
keep them and lose your life—which brings
sorrow and pain more near?

Thus we may see,
who cleaves to fame
rejects what is more great;
who loves large stores
gives up the richer state.

Who is content
Needs fear no shame.
Who knows to stop
incurs no blame.
From danger free
long live shall he.

名與身孰親。身與貨孰多。得與亡孰病。是故甚愛必

45 *Great or Overflowing Virtue*

大成若缺。其用不弊。大盈若沖其用不窮大直若屈。

Who thinks his great achievements poor
shall find his vigor long endure.
Of greatest fullness, deemed a void,
exhaustion ne'er shall stem the tide.

Do thou what's straight still crooked deem;
thy greatest art still stupid seem,
and eloquence a stammering scream.

Constant action overcomes cold; being still overcomes heat.

Purity and stillness give the correct law to all under Heaven.

The

farther

that

one goes

out from

himself

the less

he knows.

Breath

46 The Moderating of Desire or Ambition

天下有道、郤走馬以糞。天下無道、戎馬生於郊。禍莫

When the Tao prevails in the world, they send back their swift horses to draw the dung-carts. When the Tao is disregarded in the world, the war-horses breed in the border lands.

There is no guilt greater than to sanction ambition; no calamity greater than to be discontented with one's lot; no fault greater than the wish to be getting. Therefore, the sufficiency of contentment is an enduring and unchanging sufficiency.

47 Surveying What is Far-Off

不出戶、知天下。不闚牖見天道。其出彌遠、其知彌少。

Without going outside his door, one understands all that takes place under the sky; without looking out from his window, one sees the Tao of Heaven. The farther that one goes out from himself, the less he knows.

Therefore, the sages got their knowledge without traveling; gave their right names to things without seeing them; and accomplished their ends without any purpose of doing so.

48 Forgetting Knowledge

為學日益為道日損損之又損以至於無為無為而

He who devotes himself to learning seeks from day to day to increase his knowledge; he who devotes himself to the Tao seeks from day to day to diminish his doing.

He diminishes it and again diminishes it, till he arrives at doing nothing on purpose. Having arrived at this point of non-action, there is nothing which he does not do.

He who gets as his own all under Heaven does so by giving himself no trouble with that end. If one take trouble with that end, he is not equal to getting as his own all under Heaven.

49 The Quality of Indulgence

聖人無常心以百姓心為心善者吾善之不善者吾

The Sage has no invariable mind of his own; he makes the mind of the people his mind.

To those who are good to me, I am good; and to those who are not good to me, I am also good; and thus all get to be good. To those who are sincere with me, I am sincere; and to those who are not sincere with me, I am also sincere; and thus all get to be sincere.

The Sage has in the world an appearance of indecision, and keeps his mind in a state of indifference to all. The people all keep their eyes and ears directed to him, and he deals with them all as his children.

50 The Value Set on Life

出生入死。生之徒十有三死之徒十有三人之生動

Men come forth and live; they enter again and die.

Of every ten, three are ministers of life to themselves; and three are ministers of death.

There are also three in every ten whose aim is to live, but whose movements tend to the land or place of death. And for what reason? Because of their excessive endeavors to perpetuate life.

But I have heard that he who is skillful in managing the life entrusted to him for a time travels on the land without having to shun rhinoceros or tiger, and enters a host without having to avoid buff coat or sharp weapon. The rhinoceros finds no place in him into which to thrust its horn, nor the tiger a place in which to fix its claws, nor the weapon a place to admit its point. And for what reason? Because there is in him no place of death.

51 The Operation of the Tao in Nourishing Things

道生之。德畜之。物形之勢成之。是以萬物莫不尊

All things are produced by the Tao, and nourished by its outflowing operation. They receive their forms according to the nature of each, and are completed according to the circumstances of their condition. Therefore, all things without exception honor the Tao and exalt its outflowing operation. This honoring of the Tao and exalting of its operation is not the result of any ordination, but always a spontaneous tribute.

Thus it is that the Tao produces all things, nourishes them, brings them to their full growth, nurses them, completes them, matures them, maintains them, and overspreads them. It produces them and makes no claim to the possession of them; it carries them through their processes and does not vaunt its ability in doing so; it brings them to maturity and exercises no control over them; this is called its mysterious operation.

52 *Returning to the Source*

天下有始以爲天下母。既得其母以知其子。既知

The Tao, which originated all under the sky, is to be considered as the mother of them all. When the mother is found, we know what her children should be. When one knows that he is his mother's child, and proceeds to guard the qualities of the mother that belong to him, to the end of his life he will be free from all peril.

Let him keep his mouth closed, and shut up the portals of his nostrils, and all his life he will be exempt from laborious exertion. Let him keep his mouth open, and spend his breath in the promotion of his affairs, and all his life there will be no safety for him.

The perception of what is small is the secret of clear-sightedness; the guarding of what is soft and tender is the secret of strength.

Who uses well his light,
reverting to its source so bright,
will from his body ward all blight,
and hide the unchanging from men's sight.

53 *Increase of Evidence*

使
我
介
然
有
知
行
於
大
道
唯
施
是
畏
大
道
甚
夷
而

If I were suddenly to become known, and put into a position to conduct a government according to the Great Tao, what I should be most afraid of would be a boastful display.

The great Tao, or way, is very level and easy; but people love the byways.

Their courtyards and buildings shall be well kept, but their fields shall be ill-cultivated, and their granaries very empty. They shall wear elegant and ornamented robes, carry a sharp sword at their girdle, pamper themselves in eating and drinking, and have a superabundance of property and wealth; such princes may be called robbers and boasters. This is contrary to the Tao, surely!

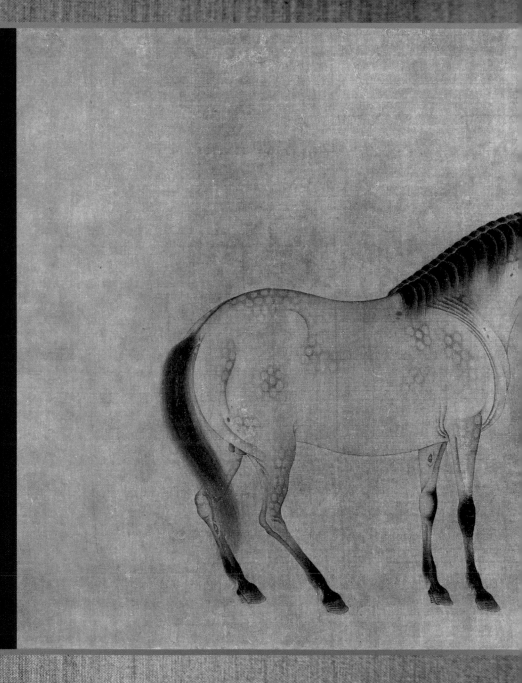

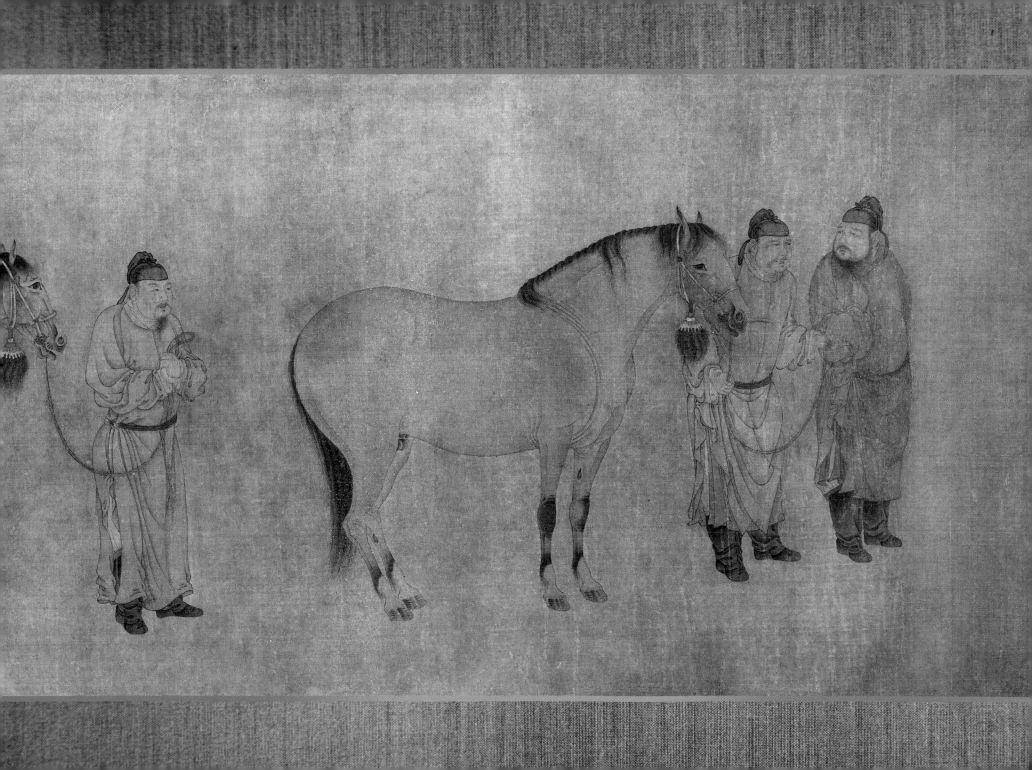

54 The Cultivation of the Tao, and the Observation of Its Effects

善建者不拔。善抱者不脫子孫以祭祀不輟。修之於

What Tao's skillful planter plants
can never be uptorn;
What his skillful arms enfold,
from him can ne'er be borne.
Sons shall bring in lengthening line,
sacrifices to his shrine.

Tao when nursed within one's self,
his vigor will make true;
and where the family it rules
what riches will accrue!
The neighborhood where it prevails
in thriving will abound;
and when 'tis seen throughout the state,
good fortune will be found.
Employ it the kingdom o'er,
and men thrive all around.

In this way the effect will be seen in the person, by
the observation of different cases; in the family; in
the neighborhood; in the state; and in the kingdom.

How do I know that this effect is sure to hold thus all
under the sky? By this method of observation.

He

who

knows

the Tao

does not

care

to speak

about it.

Revolve

55 *The Mysterious Charm*

含德之厚比於赤子蜂蠆虺蛇不螫猛獸不據攫鳥

He who has in himself abundantly the attributes of the Tao is like an infant. Poisonous insects will not sting him; fierce beasts will not seize him; birds of prey will not strike him. The infant's bones are weak and its sinews soft, but yet its grasp is firm. It knows not yet the union of male and female, and yet its virile member may be excited, showing the perfection of its physical essence. All day long it will cry without its throat becoming hoarse, showing the harmony in its constitution.

To him by whom this harmony is known,
the secret of the unchanging Tao is shown,
and in the knowledge wisdom finds its throne.
All life-increasing arts to evil turn;
where the mind makes the vital breath to burn,
false is the strength, and o'er it we should mourn.

When things have become strong, they then become old, which may be said to be contrary to the Tao. Whatever is contrary to the Tao soon ends.

56 The Mysterious Excellence

He who knows the Tao does not care to speak about it; he who is ever ready to speak about it does not know it.

He who knows it will keep his mouth shut and close his nostrils. He will blunt his sharp points and unravel the complications of things; he will temper his brightness, and bring himself into agreement with the obscurity of others. This is called "the Mysterious Agreement."

Such a one cannot be treated familiarly or distantly; he is beyond all consideration of profit or injury, of nobility or meanness. He is the noblest man under Heaven.

知者不言、言者不知。塞其兌、閉其門。挫其銳、解其分。

義之摩詰千載書畫之絕戲翰墨

鵲華云按輿志諸書載名勝
向以絹孟頫是圖珍為祕寶每一展覺
神為馳往茲僅於寒齋得一寓目於
少之午夏二月東巡狩謁關里岱宗
禮成授輯陽周冕珠燁雲東北隅諸
山詢之守土大夫乃卷西項高丘銳者
為華不注迤西兩項以厚者為鵲山向
固東之刻即巴命郵報陸京齋吳興畫
卷向來考校而謹合風景葢天假
之緣嘗誤偶裁此但吳興自記云東為
舒亮惟較之圖幸以目親葢在蒲西豈
一呵手誤欲故書迫此鵲華一圖多於其山
之側蓋藏於氏云戊辰清明日偶華

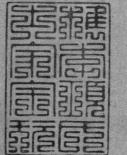

余二十年前見此圖於嘉興項氏以為文敏一生得意
筆不減伯時蓮社圖每任來於懷七年長至日項
晦伯以偏舟訪余攜此卷晃余則走社之先在焉上
互相展視出此晦伯日不可使延津之劍久判
雖雄蓮屬余藏之我鴻...書為記 壬寅除夕

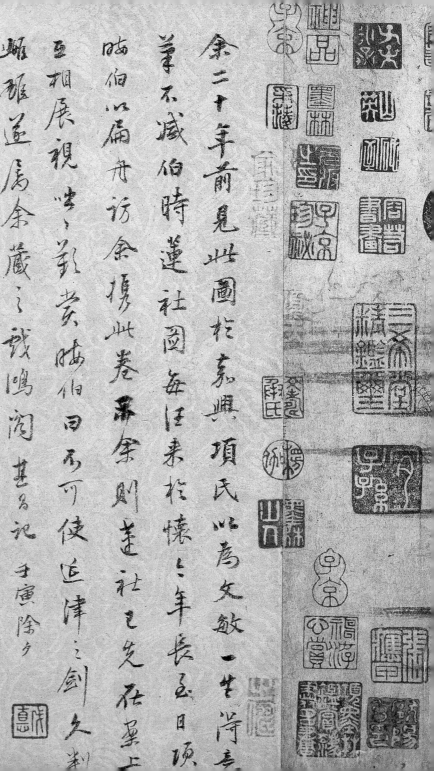

萬卉何慚繡後塵蜂喧蝶誑

57 *The Genuine Influence*

A state may be ruled by measures of correction; weapons of war may be used with crafty dexterity; but the kingdom is made one's own only by freedom from action and purpose. How do I know that it is so? By these facts:

In the kingdom the multiplication of prohibitive enactments increases the poverty of the people; the more implements the people have to add to their profit the greater disorder there is in the state and clan; the more acts of crafty dexterity that men possess, the more do strange contrivances appear; the more display there is of legislation, the more thieves and robbers there are.

Therefore, a Sage has said: "I will do nothing of purpose, and the people will be transformed of themselves; I will be fond of keeping still, and the people will of themselves become correct. I will take no trouble about it, and the people will of themselves become rich; I will manifest no ambition, and the people will of themselves attain to the primitive simplicity."

以正治國以奇用兵以無事取天下吾何以

北遇暫得於己快然自足不
知老之將至及其所之既惓情
隨事遷感慨係之矣向之
欣俛仰之間以為陳迹猶
能不以之興懷況修短隨化終
期於盡古人云死生亦大矣豈
痛哉每攬昔人興感之由
合一契未嘗不臨文嗟悼
能喻之於懷固知一死生為虛
誕齊彭殤為妄作後之視
亦由今之視昔悲夫故
列叙時人錄其所述雖世殊事
異所以興懷其致一也後之攬
者亦將有感於斯文

永和九年歲在癸丑暮春之初會于會稽山陰之蘭亭脩禊事也群賢畢至少長咸集此地有崇山峻領茂林脩竹又有清流激湍映帶左右引以為流觴曲水列坐其次雖無絲竹管弦之盛一觴一詠亦足以暢敘幽情是日也天朗氣清惠風和暢仰觀宇宙之大俯察品類之盛所以遊目騁懷足以極視聽之娛信可樂也夫人之相與俯仰一世或取諸懷抱悟言一室之內或因寄所託放浪形骸之外

58 Transformation According to Circumstances

The government that seems the most unwise,
oft goodness to the people best supplies;
that which is meddling, touching everything,
will work but ill, and disappointment bring.

Misery! Happiness is to be found by its side! Happiness!
Misery lurks beneath it! Who knows what either will come
to in the end? Shall we then dispense with correction?
The method of correction shall by a turn become distortion,
and the good in it shall by a turn become evil. The delusion
of the people on this point has indeed subsisted for a
long time.

Therefore, the Sage is like a square which cuts no one with
its angles; like a corner which injures no one with its
sharpness. He is straightforward, but allows himself no
license; he is bright, but does not dazzle.

其政悶悶其民淳淳。其政察察其民缺缺。禍兮福之

59 Guarding the Tao

治
人
事
天
莫
若
嗇。
夫
唯
嗇、
是
謂
早
服。
早
服
謂
之
重
積

For regulating the human in our constitution and rendering the proper service to the heavenly, there is nothing like moderation. It is only by this moderation that there is effected an early return to man's normal state. That early return is what I call the repeated accumulation of the attributes of the Tao. With that repeated accumulation of those attributes, there comes the subjugation of every obstacle to such return. Of this subjugation we know not what shall be the limit; and when one knows not what the limit shall be, he may be the ruler of a state.

He who possesses the mother of the state may continue long. His case is like that of the plant of which we say that its roots are deep and its flower stalks firm: this is the way to secure that its enduring life shall long be seen.

60 Occupying the Throne

治
大
國
若
烹
小
鮮。
以
道
莅
天
下、
其
鬼
不
神。
非
其
鬼
不

Governing a great state is like cooking small fish.

Let the kingdom be governed according to the Tao, and the manes of the departed will not manifest their spiritual energy. It is not that those manes have not that spiritual energy, but it will not be employed to hurt men. It is not that it could not hurt men, but neither does the ruling Sage hurt them. When these two do not injuriously affect each other, their good influences converge in the virtue of the Tao.

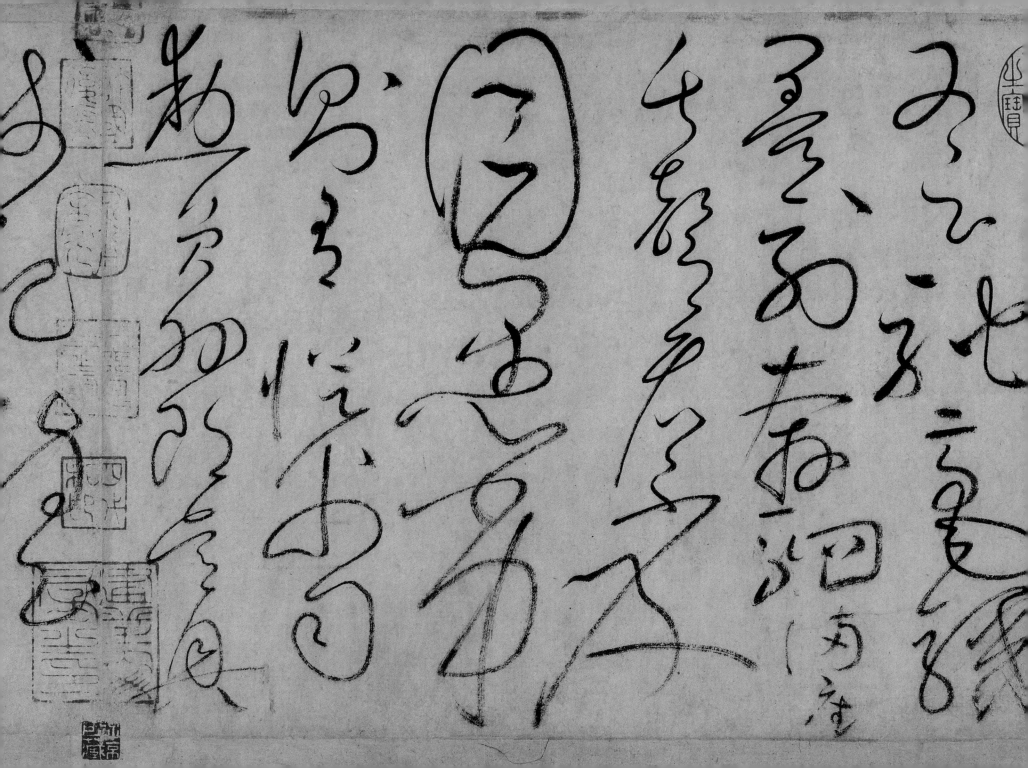

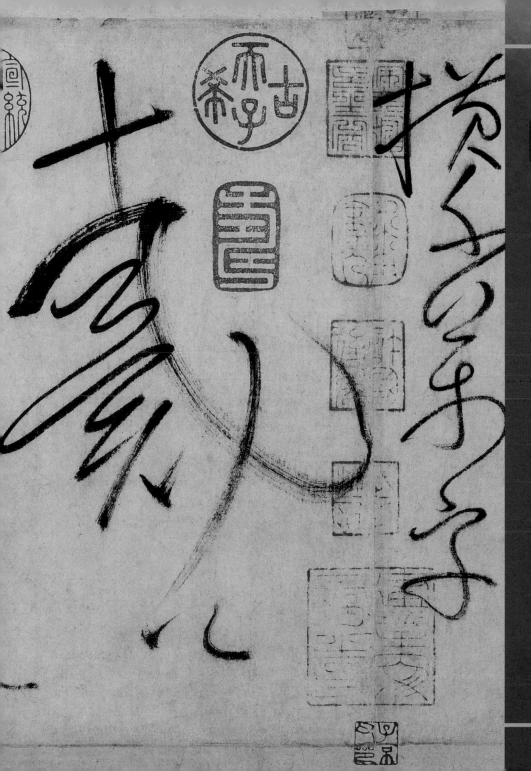

61 *The Attribute of Humility*

大國者下流。天下之交。天下之牝。牝常以靜勝牡。

What makes a great state is its being like a low-lying, down-flowing stream; it becomes the center to which tend all the small states under Heaven.

To illustrate from the case of all females: The female always overcomes the male by her stillness. Stillness may be considered a sort of abasement.

Thus it is that a great state, by condescending to small states, gains them for itself; and that small states, by abasing themselves to a great state, win it over to them. In the one case the abasement leads to gaining adherents, in the other case to procuring favor.

The great state only wishes to unite men together and nourish them; a small state only wishes to be received by, and to serve, the other. Each gets what it desires, but the great state must learn to abase itself.

62 Practicing the Tao

Tao has of all things the most honored place.
No treasures give good men so rich a grace;
bad men it guards, and doth their ill efface.

Its admirable words can purchase honor; its admirable deeds can raise their performer above others. Even men who are not good are not abandoned by it.

Therefore, when the sovereign occupies his place as the Son of Heaven, and he has appointed his three ducal ministers, though a prince were to send in a round symbol-of-rank large enough to fill both the hands, and that as the precursor of the team of horses in the court-yard, such an offering would not be equal to a lesson of this Tao, which one might present on his knees.

Why was it that the ancients prized this Tao so much? Was it not because it could be got by seeking for it, and the guilty could escape from the stain of their guilt by it? This is the reason why all under Heaven consider it the most valuable thing.

道者萬物之奧善人之寶不善人之所保美言

凡鍾武当度清

水流如激箭

人世感浮萍

癩屬根本

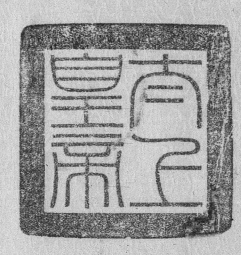

為無為。事無事。味無味。大小多小報怨以德。圖難於

63 Thinking in the Beginning

It is the way of the Tao to act without thinking of acting; to conduct affairs without feeling the trouble of them; to taste without discerning any flavor; to consider what is small as great, and a few as many; and to recompense injury with kindness.

The master of it anticipates things that are difficult while they are easy, and does things that would become great while they are small. All difficult things in the world are sure to arise from a previous state in which they were easy, and all great things from one in which they were small. Therefore, the Sage, while he never does what is great, is able on that account to accomplish the greatest things.

He who lightly promises is sure to keep but little faith; he who is continually thinking things easy is sure to find them difficult. Therefore, the Sage sees difficulty even in what seems easy, and so never has any difficulties.

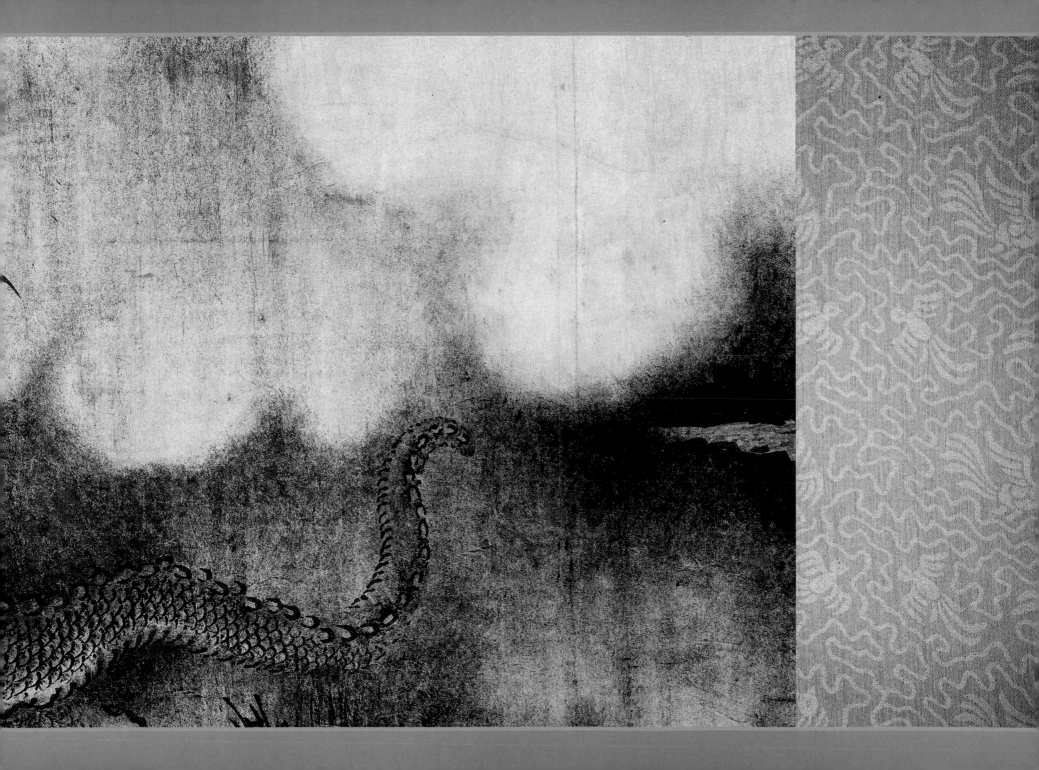

Gentleness

is

sure

to be

victorious

even in

battle.

Rhythm

64 *Guarding the Minute*

其安易持。其未兆易謀。其脆易泮。其微易散。為之

That which is at rest is easily kept hold of; before a thing has given indications of its presence, it is easy to take measures against it; that which is brittle is easily broken; that which is very small is easily dispersed.

Action should be taken before a thing has made its appearance; order should be secured before disorder has begun.

The tree which fills the arms grew from the tiniest sprout; the tower of nine stories rose from a small heap of earth; the journey of a thousand leagues commenced with a single step.

He who acts with an ulterior purpose does harm; he who takes hold of a thing in the same way loses his hold. The Sage does not act so, and therefore does no harm; he does not lay hold so, and therefore, does not lose his hold.

But people in their conduct of affairs are constantly ruining them when they are on the eve of success. If they were careful at the end, as they should be at the beginning, they would not so ruin them.

Therefore, the Sage desires what other men do not desire, and does not prize things difficult to get; he learns what other men do not learn, and turns back to what the multitude of men have passed by. Thus he helps the natural development of all things, and does not dare to act with an ulterior purpose of his own.

65 *Pure, Unmixed Excellence*

古之善爲道者非以明民將以愚之民之難治以其

The ancients who showed their skill in practicing the Tao did so not to enlighten the people, but rather to make them simple and ignorant.

The difficulty in governing the people arises from their having much knowledge. He who tries to govern a state by his wisdom is a scourge to it; while he who does not try to do so is a blessing.

He who knows these two things finds in them also his model and rule. Ability to know this model and rule constitutes what we call the mysterious excellence of a governor. Deep and far-reaching is such mysterious excellence, showing indeed its possessor as opposite to others, but leading them to a great conformity to him.

五色鸚鵡來自嶺表養之禁
籞馴服可愛飛鳴自適往來
於苑囿間方中春繁杏遍開
翔翥其上雅詫容與自有一
種態度縱目觀之宛勝圖畫
因賦是詩焉

天產乾皋此異禽
遐陬來貢九重深
體全五色非凡質
惠吐多言更好音
飛翥似憐毛羽貴
徘徊如飽稻粱心
緗膺紺趾誠端雅
爲賦新篇步武吟

製　并書

66 *Putting One's Self Last*

江海所以能爲百谷王者以其善下之故能

That whereby the rivers and seas are able to receive the homage and tribute of all the valley streams, is their skill in being lower than they; it is thus that they are the kings of them all.

So it is that the sage ruler, wishing to be above men, puts himself by his words below them, and, wishing to be before them, places his person behind them.

In this way, though he has his place above them, men do not feel his weight, nor though he has his place before them, do they feel it an injury to them. Therefore all in the world delight to exalt him and do not weary of him.

Because he does not strive, no one finds it possible to strive with him.

67 Three Precious Things

天下皆謂我道大似不肖夫唯大故似不肖若

All the world says that, while my Tao is great, it yet appears to be inferior to other systems of teaching. Now it is just its greatness that makes it seem to be inferior. If it were like any other system, for long would its smallness have been known!

But I have three precious things which I prize and hold fast. The first is gentleness; the second is economy; and the third is shrinking from taking precedence of others.

With that gentleness I can be bold; with that economy I can be liberal; shrinking from taking precedence of others, I can become a vessel of the highest honor.

Nowadays they give up gentleness and are all for being bold; economy, and are all for being liberal; the hindmost place, and seek only to be foremost; of all which end in death.

Gentleness is sure to be victorious even in battle, and firmly to maintain its ground. Heaven will save its possessor, by his very gentleness protecting him.

68 *Matching Heaven*

善爲士者不武。善戰者不怒善勝敵者不與善用人

He who in Tao's wars has skill
assumes no martial port;
he who fights with most good will
to rage makes no resort.
He who vanquishes yet still
keeps from his foes apart;
he whose hests men most fulfill
yet humbly plies his art.

Thus we say, "He ne'er contends,
and therein is his might."
Thus we say, "Men's wills he bends,
That they with him unite."
Thus we say, "Like Heaven's his ends,
No Sage of old more bright."

昔人多畫歲寒三友予獨取此三種愛
其有凌寒之姿雖雪霜嚴摧剝未遽
丰韻後凋何愧焉因補畫此
同此之賞 白雲谿史壽平

69　The Use of the Mysterious Tao

用兵有言。吾不敢爲主而爲客。不敢進寸而退尺。是

A master of the art of war has said, "I do not dare to be the host to commence the war; I prefer to be the guest to act on the defensive. I do not dare to advance an inch; I prefer to retire a foot."

This is called marshalling the ranks where there are no ranks; baring the arms to fight where there are no arms to bare; grasping the weapon where there is no weapon to grasp; advancing against the enemy where there is no enemy.

There is no calamity greater than lightly engaging in war. To do that is near losing the gentleness which is so precious. Thus it is that when opposing weapons are actually crossed, he who deplores the situation conquers.

70　The Difficulty of Being Rightly Known

吾言甚易知甚易行。天下莫能知莫能行。言有宗事

My words are very easy to know, and very easy to practice; but there is no one in the world who is able to know and able to practice them.

There is an originating and all-comprehending principle in my words, and an authoritative law for the things which I enforce.

It is because they do not know these,
that men do not know me.

They who know me are few,
and I am on that account the more to be prized.

It is thus that the Sage wears a poor garb of hair cloth,
while he carries his signet of jade in his bosom.

71 The Disease of Knowing

知
不
知
上
不
知
知
病
夫
唯
病
病
是
以
不
病
聖
人
不
病

To know and yet think we do not know is the highest attainment; not to know and yet think we do know is a disease.

It is simply by being pained at the thought of having this disease that we are preserved from it. The Sage has not the disease. He knows the pain that would be inseparable from it, and therefore, he does not have it.

72 Loving One's Self

民
不
畏
威
則
大
威
至
無
狎
其
所
居
無
厭
其
所
生
夫
唯

When the people do not fear what they ought to fear, that which is their great dread will come on them.

Let them not thoughtlessly indulge themselves in their ordinary life; let them not act as if weary of what that life depends on. It is by avoiding such indulgence that such weariness does not arise.

Therefore, the Sage knows these things of himself, but does not parade his knowledge; loves, but does not appear to set a value on, himself. And thus he puts the latter alternative away and makes choice of the former.

Man

at his birth

is supple

and weak;

at his death,

firm and strong.

So it is with

all things.

Strength

73 *Allowing Men to Take Their Course*

勇
於
敢
則
殺
。
勇
於
不
敢
則
活
。
此
兩
者
或
利
或
害
。
天
之

He whose boldness appears in his daring to do wrong, in defiance of the laws, is put to death; he whose boldness appears in his not daring to do so lives on. Of these two cases the one appears to be advantageous, and the other to be injurious. But when Heaven's anger smites a man, who the cause shall truly scan? On this account the Sage feels a difficulty as to what to do in the former case.

It is the way of Heaven not to strive, and yet it skillfully overcomes; not to speak, and yet it is skillful in obtaining a reply; does not call, and yet men come to it of themselves. Its demonstrations are quiet, and yet its plans are skillful and effective.

The meshes of the net of Heaven are large; far apart, but letting nothing escape.

74 Restraining Delusion

民不畏死。奈何以死懼之。若使民常畏死而為奇者

The people do not fear death; to what purpose is it to try to frighten them with death?

If the people were always in awe of death, and I could always seize those who do wrong, and put them to death, who would dare to do wrong?

There is always One who presides over the infliction death. He who would inflict death in the room of him who so presides over it may be described as hewing wood for a great carpenter. Seldom is it that he who undertakes the hewing, instead of the great carpenter, does not cut his own hands!

75 How Greediness Injures

民之饑以其上食稅之多是以饑。民之難治以其上

The people suffer from famine because of the multitude of taxes consumed by their superiors. It is through this that they suffer famine.

The people are difficult to govern because of the excessive agency of their superiors in governing them. It is through this that they are difficult to govern.

The people make light of dying because of the greatness of their labors in seeking for the means of living. It is this which makes them think light of dying.

Thus it is that to leave the subject of living altogether out of view is better than to set a high value on it.

人之生也柔弱其死也堅強萬物草木之生也柔脆。

76 *A Warning Against Trusting in Strength*

Man at his birth is supple and weak; at his death, firm and strong. So it is with all things. Trees and plants, in their early growth, are soft and brittle; at their death, dry and withered.

Thus it is that firmness and strength are the concomitants of death; softness and weakness, the concomitants of life.

Hence he who relies on the strength of his forces does not conquer; and a tree which is strong will fill the outstretched arms, and thereby invites the feller.

Therefore, the place of what is firm and strong is below, and that of what is soft and weak is above.

77 *The Way of Heaven*

天之道其猶張弓與。高者抑之下者舉之。有餘者損

May not the Way, or Tao, of Heaven be compared to the method of bending a bow? The part of the bow which was high is brought low, and what was low is raised up. So Heaven diminishes where there is superabundance, and supplements where there is deficiency.

It is the Way of Heaven to diminish superabundance, and to supplement deficiency. It is not so with the way of man. He takes away from those who have not enough to add to his own superabundance.

Who can take his own superabundance and therewith serve all under Heaven? Only he who is in possession of the Tao!

Therefore, the ruling Sage acts without claiming the results as his; he achieves his merit and does not rest arrogantly in it: he does not wish to display his superiority.

78 Things to Be Believed

天下莫柔弱於水。而攻堅强者莫之能勝。其無以易

There is nothing in the world more soft and weak than
water, and yet for attacking things that are firm and strong
there is nothing that can take preced   ence of it; for there
is nothing so effectual for which it can be changed.
Every one in the world knows that the soft overcomes
the hard, and the weak the strong, but no one is able to
carry it out in practice.

Therefore, a Sage has said,
"He who accepts his state's reproach,
is hailed therefore its altars' lord;
to him who bears men's direful woes
they all the name of King accord."

Words that are strictly true seem to be paradoxical.

79 Adherence to Bond or Covenant

和大怨必有餘怨。安可以爲善。是以聖人執左契而

When a reconciliation is effected between two parties after
a great animosity, there is sure to be a grudge remaining in
the mind of the one who was wrong. And how can this be
beneficial to the other?

Therefore, to guard against this, the Sage keeps the
left-hand portion of the record of the engagement,
and does not insist on the speedy fulfillment of it by the
other party. So, he who has the attributes of the Tao regards
only the conditions of the engagement, while he who has
not those attributes regards only the conditions favorable
to himself. In the Way of Heaven, there is no partiality of
love; it is always on the side of the good man.

80 *Standing Alone*

In a little state with a small population, I would so order it, that, though there were individuals with the abilities of ten or a hundred men, there should be no employment of them; I would make the people, while looking on death as a grievous thing, yet not remove elsewhere to avoid it.

Though they had boats and carriages, they should have no occasion to ride in them; though they had buff coats and sharp weapons, they should have no occasion to don or use them.

I would make the people return to the use of knotted cords instead of the written characters. They should think their coarse food sweet; their plain clothes beautiful; their poor dwellings places of rest; and their common simple ways sources of enjoyment.

There should be a neighboring state within sight, and the voices of the fowls and dogs should be heard all the way from it to us, but I would make the people to old age, even to death, not have any intercourse with it.

小國寡民。使有什伯之器而不用使民重死而

81 *The Manifestation of Simplicity*

信言不美。美言不信。善者不辯。辯者不善。知者不

Sincere words are not fine; fine words are not sincere. Those who are skilled in the Tao do not dispute about it; the disputatious are not skilled in it. Those who know the Tao are not extensively learned; the extensively learned do not know it.

The Sage does not accumulate for himself. The more that he expends for others, the more does he possess of his own; the more that he gives to others, the more does he have himself.

With all the sharpness of the Way of Heaven, it injures not; with all the doing in the way of the Sage he does not strive.

Credits

The following image credits correspond to the order in which art appears in this volume. Numbers preceding the credits are provided strictly for sequencing purposes.

1. Front endpaper: Formerly attributed to Chen Rong (ca. 1200-1266). *Dragon and Tiger* (detail). Chinese, Southern Song Dynasty (1127-1279), second half of 13th century. Ink on silk (57 x 38 ¼ in.). Museum of Fine Arts, Boston, William Sturgis Bigelow Collection (11.6162). Photograph © Museum of Fine Arts, Boston.

2. Qiu Ying (1494/1495-1552). *Saying Farewell at Xunyan*, (detail). Chinese, Ming Dynasty (1368-1644). Handscroll, ink and full color on paper (length 13 ¼ in.). The Nelson-Atkins Museum of Art, Kansas City, Missouri. Purchase: Nelson Trust (46-50). Photograph © John Lamberton/The Nelson-Atkins Museum of Art.

3. Chen Rong (ca. 1200-1266). *Five Dragons* (detail). Chinese, Southern Song Dynasty (1127-1279). Handscroll, ink on paper (13 ½ x 23 ½ in.). The Nelson-Atkins Museum of Art, Kansas City, Missouri. Purchase: Nelson Trust (48-15). Photograph © John Lamberton/The Nelson-Atkins Museum of Art.

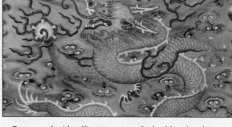

4. Dragon robe (detail), 1736-1795. Embroidered satin brocade (length 56 ¾ in.). The Minneapolis Institute of Arts, John R. Van Derlip Fund (41.74.11). Photograph © The Minneapolis Institute of Arts.

5. Chiang Shen (ca.1090-1138), *Verdant Mountains* (detail). Chinese, Northern Song Dynasty (960-1279). Handscroll, ink and full color on paper (12 ¹⁄₁₆ x 116 ½ in.). The Nelson-Atkins Museum of Art, Kansas City, Missouri. Purchase: Nelson Trust (53-49). Photograph © John Lamberton/The Nelson-Atkins Museum of Art.

6. Qiu Ying (1494/1495-1552). *Saying Farewell at Xunyang* (detail). Chinese, Ming Dynasty (1368-1644). Handscroll, ink and full color on paper (length 13 ¼ in.). The Nelson-Atkins Museum of Art, Kansas City, Missouri. Purchase: Nelson Trust (46-50). Photograph © John Lamberton/The Nelson-Atkins Museum of Art.

7. Rubbing made from the back of a votive stone sculpture: Taoist stele depicting Lao Tzu with two attendants showing profile. Six Dynasties (222-589): Northern Wei Dynasty (386-534), 500. © The Field Museum, Chicago, Illinois A108893_19.

8. Chen Rong (ca. 1200-1266). *Nine Dragons* (detail). Chinese, Southern Song Dynasty (1127-1279), 1244. Ink and color on paper (18 ¼ x 431 ⅝ in.). Museum of Fine Arts, Boston, Francis Gardner Curtis Fund (17.1697). Photograph © 2008 Museum of Fine Arts, Boston.

9. Taoist robe (detail), 1821-1850. Silk (54 x 49 in.). The Minneapolis Institute of Arts, John R. Van Derlip Fund (42.8.302). Photograph © The Minneapolis Institute of Arts.

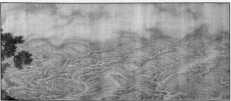

10. Zhou Chen (1450-1535). *The North Sea* (detail). Chinese, Ming Dynasty (1368-1644). Handscroll, ink and light color on silk (11 ⅛ X 53 ½ in.). The Nelson-Atkins Museum of Art, Kansas City, Missouri. Purchase: Nelson Trust (58-55). Photograph © Mel McLean/The Nelson-Atkins Museum of Art.

11. Copy after Zhou Fang (active 766-796). *Palace Ladies Tuning the Lute* (detail). Chinese, Tang Dynasty (618-907), 12th century copy. Handscroll, ink and color on silk (11 x 29 ⅝ in.). The Nelson-Atkins Museum of Arts, Kansas City, Missouri. Purchase: Nelson Trust (32-159/1). Photograph © John Lamberton/The Nelson-Atkins Museum of Art.

12. *Queen of Paradise* (detail). Chinese scroll painting. Musée National des Arts Asiatiques-Guimet, Paris (Inv.: EO 717). Photograph © Thierry Ollivier/Réunion des Musées Nationaux/Art Resource.

13. Yan Hongzi. *Daoist Deity of Earth and His Retinue* (detail). Chinese, Qing Dynasty (1644-1911). Ink on paper (20 x 229 ¾ in.). Museum of Fine Arts, Boston, Keith McLeod Fund (57.686., SC 199226). Photograph © 2008 Museum of Fine Arts, Boston.

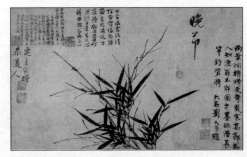

14. Ku An. *Bamboo in Monochrome Ink*. The National Palace Museum, Taipei, Taiwan, Republic of China.

15. *Daoist Sutra: The Three Deities of Heaven, Earth, and Water* (detail). Chinese, Ming Dynasty (1368-1644), dated 1470. Album, gold on indigo paper (12 x 4 ⁵⁄₁₆ in.). Museum of Fine Arts, Boston, Asiatic Curator's Fund and Frederick L. Jack Fund (1996.58). Photograph © Museum of Fine Arts, Boston.

16. Chen Rong (ca. 1200-1266). *Nine Dragons* (detail). Chinese, Southern Song Dynasty (1127-1279), 1244. Ink and color on paper (18 ¼ X 431 ⅝ in.). Museum of Fine Arts, Boston, Francis Gardner Curtis Fund (17.1697). Photograph © 2008 Museum of Fine Arts, Boston.

17. Taoist priest's robe (detail), late 18th century. Embroidered and appliquéd satin. The Minneapolis Institute of Arts, the John R. Van Derlip Fund (41.74.1). Photograph © The Minneapolis Institute of Arts.

18. Emperor Huizong (1082-1135). *Finches and Bamboo* (detail), ca. 1101-1125. Handscroll, ink and color on silk (13 ¼ X 330 ⁵⁄₁₆ in.). The Metropolitan Museum of Art, John M. Crawford, Jr., Collection, Purchase, Douglas Dillon Gift, 1981 (1981.278). Image © The Metropolitan Museum of Art/Art Resource.

19. Zhou Fang (active 730-800). *Palace Women Playing Double Sixes*. Chinese, Tang Dynasty (618-907). Handscroll, ink and color on silk. The National Palace Museum, Taipei, Taiwan, Republic of China.

20. Yan Hongzi. *Daoist Deity of Earth and His Retinue* (detail). Chinese, Qing Dynasty (1644-1911). Ink on paper (20 x 229 ¾ in.). Museum of Fine Arts, Boston, Keith McLeod Fund (57.686., SC 199225). Photograph © 2008 Museum of Fine Arts, Boston.

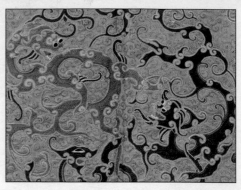

21. Li Song (active 1190-1230). *Tang Emperor Watching a Cockfight.* Chinese, Southern Song Dynasty (1127-1279). Album leaf, ink and slight color on silk (9 ¼ x 8 ¼ in.). The Nelson-Atkins Museum of Art, Kansas City, Missouri. Purchase: Nelson Trust (59-17). Photograph © Jamison Miller/The Nelson-Atkins Museum of Art.

24. *Bird on a Flowering Branch* (detail). Chinese, Southern Song Dynasty (1127-1279), 12th century. Album leaf mounted as a hanging scroll; ink and color on silk (9 ⅓ x 9 ⅔ in.). The Cleveland Museum of Art, The Kelvin Smith Collection, given by Mrs. Kelvin Smith (1985.371). Photograph © The Cleveland Museum of Art.

27. Taoist robe (detail), 1662-1722. Satin (length 58 ½ in.). The Minneapolis Institute of Arts, the John R. Van Derlip Fund (42.8.301). Photograph © The Minneapolis Institute of Arts.

25. Liu Guandao (active ca. 1279-1300). *Whiling Away the Summer* (detail). Chinese, Yuan Dynasty (1279-1368). Handscroll, ink and light color on silk (11 ⅝ x 28 ⅛ in.). The Nelson-Atkins Museum of Art, Kansas City, Missouri. Purchase: Nelson Trust (48-5). Photograph © Jamison Miller/The Nelson-Atkins Museum of Art.

23. *Hunting Falcon Attacking a Swan* (detail). Chinese, late 13th-early 14th century, Yuan Dynasty (1279-1368). Hanging scroll (laid down on panel), ink and color on paper (69 x 41 ¾ in.). The Nelson-Atkins Museum of Art, Kansas City, Missouri. Purchase: Nelson Trust (33-86). Photograph © Mel McLean/The Nelson-Atkins Museum of Art.

28. Lintel of a tomb (detail). Chinese, Western Han Dynasty, late 1st century B.C.E. Earthenware hollow tile, ink and color on a whitened ground (overall 28 ⅞ x 94 ¾ in.). Museum of Fine Arts, Boston, Gift of C. T. Loo (25.190). Photograph © 2008 Museum of Fine Arts, Boston.

26. Chen Rong (ca. 1200-1266). *Nine Dragons* (detail). Chinese, Southern Song Dynasty (1127-1279), 1244. Ink and color on paper (18 ¼ x 431 ⅝ in.). Museum of Fine Arts, Boston, Francis Gardner Curtis Fund (17.1697). Photograph © 2008 Museum of Fine Arts, Boston.

22. Cui Bo (ca. 1024-1068). *Wild Goose on a Bank of Reeds.* Chinese, Song Dynasty (960-1279), 12th century. Fan mounted as album leaf, ink and color on silk (9 ¼ x 8 ⅝ in.). The Nelson-Atkins Museum of Art, Kansas City, Missouri. Purchase: Nelson Trust (338/3A). Photograph © John Lamberton/The Nelson-Atkins Museum of Art.

29. *Queen of Paradise* (detail). Chinese scroll painting. Musée National des Arts Asiatiques-Guimet, Paris (Inv.: EO 717). Photograph © Thierry Ollivier/Réunion des Musées Nationaux/Art Resource.

30. Qiu Ying (1494/1495-1552). *Saying Farewell at Xunyang* (detail). Chinese, Ming Dynasty (1368-1644). Handscroll, ink and full color on paper (length 13 ¼ in.) The Nelson-Atkins Museum of Art, Kansas City, Missouri. Purchase: Nelson Trust (46-50). Photograph © John Lamberton/The Nelson-Atkins Museum of Art.

31. Unidentified artist. *The Daoist Immortal Lü Dongbin Crossing Lake Dongting*. Chinese, Southern Song Dynasty (1127-1279), mid-13th century. Ink and color on silk (9 ⅛ x 8 ⅞ in.). Museum of Fine Arts, Boston, Special Chinese and Japanese Fund (17.185). Photograph © 2008 Museum of Fine Arts, Boston.

32. Attributed to Jiang Zicheng (late 14th–early 15th century). *Daoist Protector against Plague* (detail). Chinese, Ming Dynasty (1368-1644), late 14th-early 15th century. Ink and color on silk (48 ¹³/₁₆ x 26 in.). Museum of Fine Arts, Boston, Fenollosa-Weld Collection (11.4008). Photograph © Museum of Fine Arts Boston.

33. Wen Zhengming (1470-1559). *Old Pine Tree*. Chinese, late 1530s. Handscroll, ink on paper (10 ¾ x 54 ⅔ in.). The Cleveland Museum of Art, Andrew R. and Martha Holden Jennings Fund (1964.43). Photograph © The Cleveland Museum of Art.

34. Yan Hongzi. *Daoist Deity of Earth and His Retinue* (detail). Chinese, Qing Dynasty (1644-1911). Ink on paper (20 x 229 ¾ in.). Museum of Fine Arts, Boston, Keith McLeod Fund (57.686., SC 199224). Photograph © 2008 Museum of Fine Arts, Boston.

35. Chen Rong (ca. 1200-1266). *Nine Dragons* (detail). Chinese, Southern Song Dynasty (1127-1279), 1244. Ink and color on paper (18 ¼ x 431 ⅝ in.). Museum of Fine Arts, Boston, Francis Gardner Curtis Fund (17.1697). Photograph © 2008 Museum of Fine Arts, Boston.

36. Dragon robe (detail), 1736-1795. Embroidered satin brocade (length 56 ¾ in.). The Minneapolis Institute of Arts, the John R. Van Derlip Fund (41.74.11). Photograph © The Minneapolis Institute of Arts.

37. Wu Zhen (1280-1354). *Fisherman*. Chinese, Yuan Dynasty (1279-1368), ca. 1350. Handscroll, ink on paper (9 ¾ x 17 in.). The Metropolitan Museum of Art, Bequest of John M. Crawford, Jr., 1988 (1989.363.33). Photograph © Malcolm Varon/The Metropolitan Museum of Art/Art Resource.

38. *Six Fish*. Chinese, Yuan Dynasty (1279-1368), early 14th century. Ink and color on silk (39 ¹⁵/₁₆ x 19 ⁵/₁₆ in.). Museum of Fine Arts, Boston, Frederick L. Jack Fund (1984.408, SC192568). Photograph © 2008 Museum of Fine Arts, Boston.

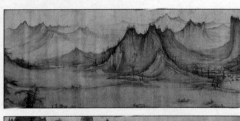

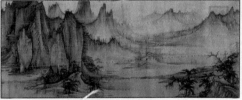

39. Xu Daoning (ca. 970-1051/1052). *Fishermen's Evening Song* (detail). Chinese, Northern Song Dynasty (960-1127), ca. 1049. Handscroll, ink and slight color on silk (19 x 82 ½ in.). The Nelson-Atkins Museum of Art, Kansas City, Missouri. Purchase: Nelson Trust (33-1559). Photograph © John Lamberton/The Nelson-Atkins Museum of Art.

40. Attributed to Laian. *Fish among Water Plants* (detail). Chinese, Yuan Dynasty (1279-1368), 14th century. Ink on silk (35 ¼ x 19 in.). Museum of Fine Arts, Boston, William Sturgis Bigelow Collection (11.6170). Photograph © 2008 Museum of Fine Arts, Boston.

41. Liu Jie. *Swimming Carp* (detail). Chinese. Hanging scroll, ink and slight color on silk (55 ½ x 34 ⅛ in.). The Cleveland Museum of Art, John L. Severance Fund (1977.55). Photograph © The Cleveland Museum of Art.

42. *The Pleasures of Fishes* (detail). Chinese, Yuan Dynasty (1279-1368), 1291. Handscroll, ink and color on paper (12 ⅛ x 233 ¾ in.). The Metropolitan Museum of Art, from the Collection of A. W. Bahr, Purchase, Fletcher Fund, 1947 (47.18.10). Photograph © The Metropolitan Museum of Art/Art Resource.

43. Li Song (active 1190-1230). *The Red Cliff (Second Excursion)*. Chinese, Southern Song Dynasty (1127-1279). Album leaf mounted as hanging scroll, ink and slight color on silk (9 ¾ x 10 ¼ in.). The Nelson-Atkins Museum of Art, Kansas City, Missouri. Purchase: Nelson Trust (49-79). Photograph © Jamison Miller/The Nelson-Atkins Museum of Art.

44. *Fish*. Chinese, Ming Dynasty (1368-1644), ca. 1400. Hanging scroll, ink and slight color on silk (13 ¾ x 21 in.). The Cleveland Museum of Art, Gift of Herbert F. Leisy in memory of his wife, Helen Stamp Leisy (1977.201). Photograph © The Cleveland Museum of Art.

45. Chen Rong (ca. 1200-1266). *Nine Dragons* (detail). Chinese, Southern Song Dynasty (1127-1279), 1244. Ink and color on paper (18 ¼ x 431 ⅝ in.). Museum of Fine Arts, Boston, Francis Gardner Curtis Fund (17.1697). Photograph © 2008 Museum of Fine Arts, Boston.

46. Taoist robe (detail). Qing Dynasty (1644-1911). Silk, cotton (56 ⅝ x 54 in.). The Minneapolis Institute of Arts, the John R. Van Derlip Fund (42.8.293). Photograph © The Minneapolis Institute of Arts.

47. *Festival of the Peaches of Longevity* (detail). Chinese, Ming Dynasty (1368-1644), 14th-15th century. Handscroll, ink, color, gold on silk (20 ½ x 188 ¹⁵⁄₁₆ in.). The Nelson-Atkins Museum of Art, Kansas City, Missouri. Gift of the Herman R. and Helen Sutherland Foundation Fund (F72-39). Photograph © Robert Newcombe/The Nelson-Atkins Museum of Art.

48. *Palace Concert*. Tang Dynasty (618-907). Hanging scroll, ink and colors on silk (19 ⅙ x 27 ⅓ in.). The National Palace Museum, Taipei, Taiwan, Republic of China.

49. *Taoist Female Immortal*. The National Palace Museum, Taipei, Taiwan, Republic of China.

50. Attributed to Emperor Huizong (1082-1135). *Court Ladies Preparing Newly Woven Silk*. Chinese, Northern Song Dynasty (960-1127), early 12th century. Ink, color, and gold on silk (14 ⁹⁄₁₆ x 57 ³⁄₁₆ in.). Museum of Fine Arts, Boston, Special Chinese and Japanese Fund (12.886). Photograph © 2008 Museum of Fine Arts, Boston.

51. *Blessings for Long-life*. Chinese hanging scroll. The National Palace Museum, Taipei, Taiwan, Republic of China.

52. Formerly attributed to Wang Juzheng (early 11th century). *Lady Watching a Maid with a Parrot.* Chinese, Southern Song Dynasty (1127-1279), early 13th century. Ink and color on silk (9 3/16 x 9 1/2 in.). Museum of Fine Arts, Boston, Harriet Otis Cruft Fund (37.302). Photograph © 2008 Museum of Fine Arts, Boston.

53. Chen Rong (ca. 1200-1266). *Nine Dragons* (detail). Chinese, Southern Song Dynasty (1127-1279), 1244. Ink and color on paper (18 1/4 x 431 5/8 in.). Museum of Fine Arts, Boston, Francis Gardner Curtis Fund (17.1697). Photograph © 2008 Museum of Fine Arts, Boston.

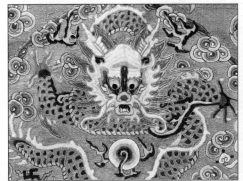

54. Taoist robe (detail), 1821-1850. Silk, (58 1/2 x 51 1/2 in.). The Minneapolis Institute of Arts, the John R. Van Derlip Fund (43.10.5). Photograph © The Minneapolis Institute of Arts.

55. *Night-Shining White* (detail). Chinese, Tang Dynasty (618-907), 8th century. Handscroll, ink on paper (12 1/8 x 13 3/8 in.). The Metropolitan Museum of Art, Purchase, The Dillon Fund Gift, 1977 (1977.78). Photograph © Malcolm Varon/The Metropolitan Museum of Art/Art Resource.

56. Traditionally attributed to Yan Liben (c. 600-673). *Northern Qi Scholars Collating Classic Texts* (detail). Chinese, Northern Song Dynasty (960-1127), 11th century. Ink and color on silk (10 7/8 x 44 7/8 in.). Museum of Fine Arts, Boston, Denman Waldo Ross Collection, 1931 (31.123). Photograph © 2008 Museum of Fine Arts Boston.

57. Chao Meng-Fu (1254-1322). *Training a Horse.* Yuan Dynasty (1279-1368). Ink on paper (9 x 19 1/4 in.). The National Palace Museum, Taipei, Taiwan, Republic of China.

58. Ren Renfa (1255-1328). *Nine Horses.* Chinese, Ming Dynasty (1368-1644), 1324. Handscroll, ink and color on silk (12 3/8 x 103 in.). The Nelson Atkins Museum of Art, Kansas City, Missouri. Purchase: Nelson Trust (49-40). Photograph © Robert Newcombe/The Nelson-Atkins Museum of Art.

59. Chao Meng-Fu (1254-1322). *Horses and Old Trees.* Yuan Dynasty (1279-1368), 1300. Hanging scroll, ink on paper (11 3/4 x 28 1/5 in.). The National Palace Museum, Taipei, Taiwan, Republic of China.

60. Chen Rong (ca. 1200-1266). *Nine Dragons* (detail) Chinese, Southern Song Dynasty (1127-1279), 1244. Ink and color on paper (18 1/4 x 431 5/8 in.). Museum of Fine Arts, Boston, Francis Gardner Curtis Fund (17.1697). Photograph © 2008 Museum of Fine Arts, Boston.

61. Taoist priest's robe (detail), 1662-1722. Embroidered satin (54 1/4 x 48 7/8 in.). The Minneapolis Institute of Arts, the John R. Van Derlip Fund (42.8.297). Photograph © The Minneapolis Institute of Arts.

62. *Festival of the Peaches of Longevity* (detail). Chinese, Ming Dynasty (1368-1644), 14th-15th century. Handscroll, ink, color, gold on silk (20 1/2 x 188 15/16 in.). The Nelson-Atkins Museum of Art, Kansas City, Missouri. Gift of the Herman R. and Helen Sutherland Foundation Fund (F72-39). Photograph © Robert Newcombe/The Nelson-Atkins Museum of Art.

63. Chao Meng-Fu (1254-1322). *Autumn Colors on the Ch'iao and Hua Mountains.* Yuan Dynasty (1279-1368). Handscroll, ink and color on paper (11 ½ x 301 ⅘ in.). The National Palace Museum, Taipei, Taiwan, Republic of China.

64. Ch'ien Hsüan. *Peonies* (detail). The National Palace Museum, Taipei, Taiwan, Republic of China.

65. Wang Fu. *Ting-wu Rubbing of the Lan-t'ing-hsu (Orchid Pavilion Preface).* Sung Dynasty (960-1279). Handscroll, ink on paper (10 ⅔ x 26 ¼ in.). The National Palace Museum, Taipei, Taiwan, Republic of China.

66. Mi Fu (1051-1107). *Mountains and Pines in Spring* (detail). Sung Dynasty (960-1279). Hanging scroll, ink and color on paper (11 ⅛ x 13 ¾ in.). The National Palace Museum, Taipei, Taiwan, Republic of China.

67. Huai-Su (active 730-770s). *Autobiography* (detail). T'ang Dynasty (618-907). Handscroll, ink on paper (11 ⅛ x 297 ¼ in.). The National Palace Museum, Taipei, Taiwan, Republic of China.

68. Huang T'ing-chien (1045-1105). *Poetry of Han-shan and Recluse P'ang* (detail). Sung Dynasty (960-1279). Album leaf, ink on paper. The National Palace Museum, Taipei, Taiwan, Republic of China.

69. Ch'ien Hsüan (1235-1300). *Squirrel on a Peach Branch* (detail). The National Palace Museum, Taipei, Taiwan, Republic of China.

70. Chen Rong (ca. 1200-1266). *Nine Dragons* (detail). Chinese, Southern Song Dynasty (1127-1279), 1244. Ink and color on paper (18 ¼ x 431 ⅝ in.). Museum of Fine Arts, Boston, Francis Gardner Curtis Fund (17.1697). Photograph © 2008 Museum of Fine Arts, Boston.

71. Taoist priest's robe (*chiang-i*) (detail), 1662-1722. Embroidered satin (length 57 ¼ in.) The Minneapolis Institute of Arts, the John R. Van Derlip Fund (42.8.300). Photograph © The Minneapolis Institute of Arts.

72. Formerly attributed to Huang Jucai (10th century). *Parrot and Insect among Pear Blossoms* (detail). Chinese, Southern Song (1127-1279) or Yuan Dynasty (1279-1368), second half of the 13th century. Ink and color on silk (10 ⅞ x 10 ⅞ in.). Museum of Fine Arts, Boston, Denman Waldo Ross Collection (30.461, SC178129). Photograph © 2008 Museum of Fine Arts, Boston.

73. Emperor Huizong (1082-1135). *Five-colored Parakeet on a Blossoming Apricot Tree* (detail). Chinese, Northern Song Dynasty (960-1127), datable to the 1110s. Ink and color on silk (21 x 49 ¼ in.). Museum of Fine Arts, Boston, Maria Antoinette Evans Fund (33.364). Photograph © 2008 Museum of Fine Arts, Boston.

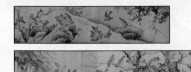

74. Attributed to Lin Liang. *A Hundred Sparrows in a Lofty Grove (Qiaolin baique tu)* (detail). Ming Dynasty (1368-1644). Handscroll, ink on silk (11 ¼ x 196 ⅛ in.). The Cleveland Museum of Art, John L. Severance Fund (1981.4). Photograph © The Cleveland Art Museum.

75. Wu Chen (1208-1354), 1350. *Bamboo in Monochrome Ink.* The National Palace Museum, Taipei, Taiwan, Republic of China.

76. Chen Shun (1483-1544). *Life Cycle of the Lotus* (detail). Chinese, Ming Dynasty (1368-1644). Handscroll, color on paper (12 x 229 ¾ in.) The Nelson-Atkins Museum of Art, Kansas City, Missouri. Purchase: Nelson Trust (31-135/34). Photograph © John Lamberton/The Nelson-Atkins Museum of Art.

77. Yun Shouping (1633-1690). *Cassia* (from *Album of Flowers*). Qing Dynasty (1644-1911). Album leaf, ink and color on paper (9 ⅝ x 11 ½ in.). The Nelson-Atkins Museum of Art, Kansas City, Missouri. Purchase: Nelson Trust (58-50/6). Photograph © Jamison Miller/The Nelson-Atkins Museum of Art.

78. Yun Shouping (1633-1690). *Pear Blossoms* (from *Album of Flowers*). Qing Dynasty (1644-1911). Album leaf, ink and color on paper (9 ⅝ x 11 ½ in.). The Nelson-Atkins Museum of Art, Kansas City, Missouri. Purchase: Nelson Trust (58-50/3). Photograph © Jamison Miller/The Nelson-Atkins Museum of Art.

79. Chen Rong (ca. 1200-1266). *Nine Dragons* (detail). Chinese, Southern Song Dynasty (1127-1279), 1244. Ink and color on paper (18 ¼ x 431 ⅝ in.). Museum of Fine Arts, Boston, Francis Gardner Curtis Fund (17.1697). Photograph © 2008 Museum of Fine Arts, Boston.

80. Taoist priest's robe (detail), 1662-1722. Silk (53 ⅜ x 48 ¾ in.). The Minneapolis Institute of Arts, the John R. Van Derlip Fund (42.8.299). Photograph © The Minneapolis Institute of Arts.

81. Taigu Yimin (unidentified artist). *Traveling Among Streams and Mountains* (detail). Chinese, Jin Dynasty (1115-1234), early to mid-13th century. Handscroll, ink on paper (15 ⅛ x 164 9/16 in.). The Nelson-Atkins Museum of Art, Kansas City, Missouri. Purchase: Kenneth A. and Helen F. Spencer Foundation Acquisition Fund (F74-35). Photograph © John Lamberton/The Nelson-Atkins Museum of Art.

82. Chen Ruyan (ca. 1331-1371). *Mountains of the Immortals* (detail). Chinese, Yuan Dynasty (1279-1368). Handscroll, ink and color on silk (length 13 ¾ in.). The Cleveland Museum of Art, Bequest of Mrs. A. Dean Perry (1997.95). Photograph © The Cleveland Museum of Art.

83. Li Shizhuo (ca. 1690-1770). *Peach Blossoms Along Rapids (T'ao-hua liu-shiu)* (detail). Chinese, Qing Dynasty (1644-1911). Album leaf, ink and water-color, silk mount (9 ½ x 5 ¾ in.). The Nelson-Atkins Museum of Art, Kansas City, Missouri. Purchase: acquired through the generosity of an anonymous donor (F78-18/8). Photograph © Jamison Miller/The Nelson-Atkins Museum of Art.

84. Li Shizhuo (ca. 1690-1770). *Imposing Overhang with Pavilion (Wei-ya t'ing-tzu)* (detail) Chinese, Qing Dynasty (1644-1911). Album leaf, ink and watercolor, silk mount (9 ½ x 5 in.). The Nelson-Atkins Museum of Art, Kansas City, Missouri. Purchase: acquired through the generosity of an anonymous donor (F78-18/12). Photograph © Jamison Miller/The Nelson Atkins Museum of Art.

85. Attributed to Qu Ding (active ca. 1023–ca. 1056). *Summer Mountains* (detail). Chinese, Northern Song Dynasty (960-1127). Handscroll, ink and light color on silk (17 ⅞ x 45 ⅜ in.). Ex coll.: C.C. Wang Family. The Metropolitan Museum of Art, New York, Gift of The Dillon Fund, 1973 (1973.120.1). Photograph © The Metropolitan Museum of Art/Art Resource.

86. Wen Zhengming (1470-1559). *The Seven Junipers.* Chinese, Ming Dynasty (1368-1644), dated 1532. Handscroll, ink on paper. The Honolulu Academy of Art, Gift of Mrs. Garter Galt, 1952 (1666.1). Photograph © The Honolulu Academy of Art.

87. Handscroll case for *The Seven Junipers.* Chinese, Ming Dynasty (1368-1644), dated 1532. The Honolulu Academy of Art, Gift of Mrs. Garter Galt, 1952 (1666.1). Photograph © The Honolulu Academy of Art.

88. Shang Hsi (active mid-1400s). *Four Immortals Conveying Longevity.* Chinese, Ming Dynasty (1368-1644). Hanging scroll, ink and colors on silk (38 ¾ x 56 ⅔ in.). The National Palace Museum, Taipei.

89. Rear endpaper: *Episode from Stories of Filial Piety* (right side of sarcophagus). Chinese, Northern Wei Dynasty (386-534), ca. 525 Limestone (24 ½ x 88 in.). The Nelson-Atkins Museum of Art, Kansas City, Missouri. Purchase: Nelson Trust (33-1543/1). Photograph © The Nelson-Atkins Museum of Art.

Front/rear cover:

Upper panel: *Episode from Stories of Filial Piety* (right side of a sarcophagus), Chinese, ca. 525, Northern Wei Dynasty (386-534). Fine, dark gray limestone (24 ¼ x 88 in.). The Nelson-Atkins Museum of Art, Kansas City, Missouri. Purchase: Nelson Trust (33-1543/1). Photograph © Jamison Miller/The Nelson-Atkins Museum of Art. (See image 89.)

Lower panel: Zhou Chen (ca. 1455-after 1536). *The North Sea* (detail). Chinese, Ming Dynasty (1368-1644). Handscroll, ink and light color on silk (11 ⅛ x 53 ½ in.). The Nelson-Atkins Museum of Art, Kansas City, Missouri. Purchase: Nelson Trust (58-55). Photograph © Mel McLean/The Nelson-Atkins Museum of Art. (See image 10.)

Azure Dragon. Roof tile (replica), Ancient Observatory, Beijing, China. Photograph © Marilyn Shea.